THE HOCKEY I LOVE

THE

HOCKEY

I LOVE

by Vladislav Tretyak

with V. Snegirev & translated by Anatole Konstantin

Lawrence Hill & Company
Westport, Connecticut

Library of Congress Cataloging in Publication Data

Tretyak, Vladislav, 1952-
  The hockey I love.

  1. Tretyak, Vladislav, 1952-   2. Hockey players—
Russia—Biography.   I. Snegirev, V., joint author.
II. Title.
GV848.5.T73A3413 1977   796.9'62'0924 (B)   77-9486
ISBN: O-88208-080-6

Published in the United States and Canada by permission of The
Copyright Agency of the USSR, Moscow.

Special thanks to Canadian sports writer Pat Hickey for his sound advice.

Special thanks to Irene Pantchenko for assistance in translation.

Jacket photograph and all others not specified below by *Abaz:*
Bochinin: pp. 48, 92, 122, 179; *Gusev:* p. 55 top; *Novosti Press Agency:* p. 52;
Panov: p. 51; *Polunin:* pp. 45, 55 bottom; *Tass: Sobolov:* p. 74;
Uspenski: pp. 80, 89.

Library of Congress Catalog Card Number: 77-9486
ISBN: O-88208-080-6

First United States edition, October, 1977.

1   2   3   4   5   6   7   8   9   10

Lawrence Hill & Company, Publishers, Inc.
Westport, Connecticut

Manufactured in the United States of America.

Table of Contents

THE HOCKEY I LOVE

Foreword

Whenever the Central Army Sports Club hockey team returns to Moscow, I am greeted first by the attendant at our Sports Palace on Leningrad Boulevard. He hands me a large package of envelopes in different sizes, shapes and colors. I scan the postmarks and find the names of many familiar cities: Leningrad, Sverdlovsk, Novosibirsk, Kharkov. There are other letters with unfamiliar stamps and postmarks from cities in Sweden, Canada, Finland and Czechoslovakia. Some letters are simply addressed "Tretyak, Moscow."

I attribute this fan mail to the increasing popularity of hockey, unquestionably due in part to the historic series between Soviet teams and professionals from the United States and Canada. In many countries, hockey has become a favorite sport, and hockey players are becoming the most popular athletes.

At home, I open the envelope and read each letter, even though I know the contents of many letters in advance. Youngsters with dreams of becoming hockey players ask me how to master all the mysteries of the sport. They ask me how to develop courage, quick reactions and endurance. They ask me how I learned to play hockey, what subjects I studied in school, how I became goaltender for the national team. They also ask about how to organize a team and how

Youngsters with dreams of becoming hockey players ask how to master the mysteries of the sport.

to build a rink. Where are goaltenders trained? How many years must you train to be chosen as goalie for a good team?

In the past my wife, Tatyana, helped me with correspondence (she is a teacher of Russian language and literature) and I faithfully attempted to answer each letter. But now there are so many letters that even the two of us cannot cope with them. The only solution is to reply to everybody at once.

How could this be done? I decided it was necessary to write a book. That book is here before you. Don't judge it too harshly. I am a goaltender, not a writer.

I will tell you about a brief period in the history of Soviet hockey—from April, 1974, through the spring of 1977. I hope to provide more than an account of specific games (journalists in the Soviet Union and North America have done that). I wish to explain, in my own words, the success of Soviet hockey and our system of training athletes and, as far as possible, to answer the questions which are most often posed to me in letters.

I will be glad if this book expands your knowledge of hockey and if, after having read it, you would like to pick up a stick and come out on the ice.

April 1974

Our train is about to leave the platform at Vyborg, the last stop before the Soviet-Finnish border. Our destination is Helsinki, the site of the 1974 world hockey championships. Hundreds of people have come to the station to greet the Soviet national team. They wish us success. They shower us with flowers and leave us with hands aching from their many handshakes.

There are schoolchildren on the platform. I am told they have skipped classes in order to say good-by to the team. I hope the teachers of Vyborg will forgive us and their pupils. We need this farewell. We need the flowers and the warm smiles.

As the train begins to move, I look at my teammates. There are many young players, en route to their first world championships. They sit quietly, but they are restless. Who said that hockey players are people without nerves?

I can understand the feelings of my teammates. Even though I am 22 years old and going to my fifth world championship, I am as excited as if it were happening for the first time.

The train runs softly over the rails. There is more than enough time to think, to reminisce. Why did I become a hockey goaltender? Was it my fate to become a goalie rather than something else? As years go by, I think of it more and more. I cannot believe it was a blind accident that helped me find my calling. But it looks as if that's what it was.

I remember once being asked what I planned to do when I graduated from school. I replied, "I would like to be a military pilot, like my father." Like most boys, I admired my father and hoped to follow his example. At the same time, I had also found a hero in hockey, a Canadian goaltender named Seth Martin.

I became involved in sports when I was very young. Our entire family was athletic. My mother was a school gym teacher and had played field hockey for a Moscow club called the Metallurgists. My older brother was a swimmer for the Dynamo club. And as a pilot, my father was aware of the importance of physical fitness and was determined that I should grow up to be strong and unafraid in difficult situations.

I was obviously fortunate to have parents who did not spoil me. To the contrary, work and discipline were part of my life from childhood. In the summers, we lived in a dacha near Moscow, and I was given difficult jobs—drawing water from the well, digging and weeding the garden and repairing things. My father was quite strict. I was punished when I failed to do my chores. At first I was hurt, but I now understand the importance of such discipline. No matter what profession one prepares for, it is important to develop good work habits. One has to start with small things like helping parents at home. I also believe that any job you begin should be done well. Perhaps these are well-known truths, but they are important to me.

For five years in a row during school vacations I joined my friends at the camps for young pioneers. Sports took up at least half our time. I ran cross-country and played table tennis and volleyball by the hour. I enjoyed all sports and wanted to be a champion in all of them.

I gladly participated in school competitions in track and field, basketball, soccer and skiing. Following my older brother's example, I tried swimming in the Dynamo club's pool, but for some reason I was always cold. I spent more time under the hot shower than I did in the pool.

Later, I became a diving enthusiast. I first jumped from a 1.5 meter trampoline without being afraid. I then moved up to the 5-meter board. From the ground, it didn't appear very high, but when I came to the edge and looked at the water, my heart stopped. I stood on the board, frozen, unable to jump. The fear grew stronger with each passing second. The height appeared to be immense and the water looked hard as stone. I knew at that moment I had to learn to overcome fear. I am still learning, but my lessons began on that 5-meter tower.

My first award in sports was a certificate of honor from the directorate of Middle School 740 for outstanding gymnastics performance in the Red Square on May 1, 1963. I will always remember that day. Thousands of children participated in the May Day celebrations in the principal square of Moscow. Dressed in identical sports uniforms, we executed complicated routines, crisply, as if we were one person. The day was cloudy and cold, but I will always remember it as a bright, exciting holiday.

In the fall I fell in love with gymnastics. I wanted to become as agile and muscular as the boys who exercised in the school gymnasium. I tried out for the gymnastics team, but my interest dimmed with the coming of winter. When the snow fell, I thought there was no better sport than cross-country skiing. Every Sunday our family skied to the Silver Forest on the outskirts of Moscow. I was the fastest skier in my class.

Then came summer and my whole life became wrapped up in soccer. I made a decision: This was it, period. I would concentrate on becoming an outstanding soccer player. I selected the famous defenseman Albert Shesternev as my idol.

But then fall came once again.

You might get the idea I was a floater, unable to stick with any one sport. But one should not forget I was only 10 years old at the time. At this age, I believe a boy may benefit from trying several sports. First of all, he acquires new skills with each sport. Secondly, he develops the self-assurance and physical conditioning to be derived from any sport. Thirdly, and I think you will probably agree with me, the wider the choice available to a youngster, the more likely he will be to find the sport right for him.

My mother conducted a class in physical fitness at the swimming pool of the Central Army Sports Club. I was attending another school at the time, but I persuaded her to take me with her one fall afternoon. Two of her students were from the club's hockey school and they had new uniforms. It seems funny today, but when I first saw those uniforms I was flabbergasted. I was envious of those boys. When we returned home that night, I told my mother: "I'm going to have a hockey uniform, too!"

When I said that, I didn't realize how difficult my task would be. The next morning, I went to the Central Army children's sports school. They were holding tryouts for young hockey players, and the competition was fierce—there were at least 20 candidates for each position. When the tryout was over, I was one of the lucky ones. I was proud and happy that the coaches had chosen me. Now I look back at those early years and I understand why I was successful in that tryout. I believe the secret lies in my chilhood when I experimented with a variety of sports and developed all-round skills.

We began training immediately—three times a week for an hour and a half. I was a forward and I worked very hard. I liked hockey but I was disappointed by one thing: more than a month had gone by and I still didn't have a uniform. I asked the coach, Vitali Yerfilov, about the uniforms and he replied, "There are not enough for everybody." I could have cried.

At that time our team had no goaltender. No one wanted to play the position, so I went to the coach and told him: "If you will give me a real uniform, I will be the goalie."

He looked at me searchingly and asked, "Aren't you afraid?"

"What is there to be afraid of?" I asked naively.

How could I have known then the pain when the puck hits the goalie? All I wanted was a hockey uniform. And I got it.

In the summer of 1967, the Central Army Sports Club team had three goaltenders: Talmachev, Tolstikov and Polupanov. Anatoli Tarasov, the senior coach, felt he needed a fourth goaltender for training sessions, and I was stunned when he selected me. I had not even dreamed of playing on Tarasov's team. The team had such famous stars as Loktev, Almetov and Alexandrov. Could a boy like myself even dare to think of joining their ranks? Imagine my state of mind that summer day when Tarasov came to our practice and said to the coach of our youth team: "Let the boy practice with the senior team." He pointed to me, and I actually froze with surprise.

That is how I began training with the famous Central Army team. It was a great honor just to practice with the team which had won so many Soviet championships and had produced more players for the Soviet national team than any other organization.

For two weeks, I was deliriously happy. Oh, how I worked. In practice, I tried desperately to stop every shot, even those on which I was hopelessly beaten. I attempted to keep up with my idols as we ran and went through our conditioning exercises.

I brought apples from our garden for my new friends. In conversation, I tried to use my idols' favorite expressions. I carried their sticks and tried to imitate them in every way. I even began walking bowlegged like Eugeni Mishakov.

And I learned from their example. "Attaboy, keep on

Soviet national hockey coach Anatoli Tarasov: "Don't listen to compliments. When they praise you, they steal from you."

trying," Tarasov told me one day as he patted me on the shoulder. This sounded like the highest praise. I already knew that our coach was stingy with compliments. He criticized and cursed much more often than he praised, afraid that compliments would go to our heads. "Don't listen to compliments," Tarasov used to say. "When they praise you, they steal from you."

My holiday ended in the middle of July. The team went south to Kudepst, and I was naturally left behind to rejoin the youth team. We had an outstanding season and became champions of Moscow. I won the award as the best junior goalie in the Soviet Union.

That winter also marked my first appearance in

international competition. The coaches of the Soviet Union's national junior team named me as their second goalie for the European union championships in Helsinki. Our performance was not considered successful. We took second place, but the national senior team had conditioned everybody to expect only victories. Any placing short of first was regarded as a failure. The following year, when the junior championships were held in Garmisch-Partenkirchen (West Germany), we won!

When we returned from the junior championships, I was summoned once again by Tarasov. "He probably wants to congratulate me," I thought, and I was surprised to find the coach staring at me with a stern expression on his face.

"And you, young man," he demanded, "why are you not on the ice? Hurry up, quickly."

I couldn't believe what I had heard. The Central Army first team was training in the rink. I ran to the locker room, changed quickly and joined my new teammates.

From that day on, my life took a new course. Tarasov set an objective for himself—to make a real goalie of me. I shared this dream, and together we began working.

I occasionally look back on those days and find it difficult to believe I was able to take the responsibility placed on my still untoughened shoulders. When I was not yet 16, I was skating three times a day. Tarasov devised new exercises specifically for me, including a few which I believed to be impossible. And then there was the MOC drill. MOC stands for maximum oxygen consumption; it has become the Central Army's trademark. Everyone skates around the rink, gradually increasing speed with each lap. Teammates told me with compassion: "Vladik, you are not going to die a natural death. This training will finish you off first."

During practice, dozens of pucks flew at my net at once, and I tried to deflect all of them. At the height of the season, I was playing almost daily—one day with the youth team; and the next day with the Central Army first team.

"During practice, dozens of pucks flew at my net at once."

If I missed even one shot, Tarasov would ask: "What happened? Let us try to figure it out." If it was my fault—and it was almost always the goalkeeper's fault—extra work was prescribed. When everyone else went home, I had to perform, let us say, a hundred attack thrusts or fifty somersaults. Since all the coaches also left, nobody would have known if I had gone home too. Yet it never occurred to me to skip even one attack thrust or a single somersault. I believed Tarasov, believed in every word he said. The coach was continuously impressing upon me that I, as an individual, did not amount to much, that my successes were the success of the whole team. I did not question him. The regimen he laid out for me was difficult, but even now I think that if things had been easier, I would not have developed all my potential. I certainly would never have been trusted with defending the Central Army Sports Club goal in the national championships—which I was at just 16.

Two years later, Coach Tarasov explained in an interview why it had been worth putting such special effort behind my training:

> *Questioner:* What do you like about this young goalie?
> *Tarasov:* First of all, his absolute eagerness and fanatic devotion to hockey. His tremendous industriousness. His uncommon abilities. He can profoundly analyze his actions; his game is thought through to the highest degree.
> *Q:* How do Tretyak's methods differ from those of other goalies?
> *T:*Vladislav maneuvers courageously and wisely; all his actions are performed with forethought.
> *Q:* Can Vladislav Tretyak become a really outstanding goalie?
> *T:* Now everything depends on him alone. The lad is 18 years old. This is the time to mature. Vladik will gradually find it easier to solve psychological and sports problems. Then he will correctly manage his fame. Personally, I think that he will be able to do it. I believe in Tretyak.

After we arrived in Helsinki, the Soviet team held a traditional Komsomol (Communist Youth League) meeting.

Volodia Petrov, the team's Komsomol organizer, chaired the meeting, and we talked about unity, mutual assistance and friendship. On these occasions, we talk bluntly, man-to-man. There is no room for sentiment. We have only one goal—to become world champions. In turn, each of my teammates discussed how we could reach this goal. I added: "I will give all my strength in order to win this championship."

In the hallway of the Polar Hotel, I found the first issue of a newspaper edited by Yuri Liapkin, one of our players. It was devoted to the national team—13 times world champions—and contained articles written by the coaches, by Petrov and by team captain Boris Mikhailov.

We were somewhat worried about the unusually large number of rookies on our team that year. They were talented young players but had not been hardened by international competition. Our coaches urged us to have courage.

That night, we played our first game—against the team from the German Democratic Republic. Our opponents were dedicated athletes. Their goalie, Hurbanek, had luck riding with him and his teammates threw themselves in front of the puck with no regard for their own safety. We won, but the game was closer than it should have been.

I had quite a difficult time even though I was not under much pressure in this game. Most of the play was in the German zone, and I never had an opportunity to get warmed up. In such circumstances, it is easy to make a mistake. I prefer it when the action is at my end of the ice. It is easier to concentrate on the puck. This is important in the world championships where the tension is tremendous and each shot is worth its weight in gold.

In my opinion we did not play well that first game. When one of our opponents was given a major penalty, we were unable to take advantage of a five-minute power play. We, the champions of the world, should have played better.

After the game, we were glad to retreat to our hotel. It was comfortable, located in the woods and isolated from the noise of the city. There was something missing at these championships, and the rookies felt it most. During the championships in Moscow, each team was hosted by young Muscovites. They showed the visiting athletes around the city, took them to the circus, organized concerts or opened their homes to the players. The same was true at the world championships in Prague—I will never forget our doting hosts from the CTZ factory in Prague. In Helsinki, the hotel staff was friendly, but we were left completely to ourselves. Aside from competition, the days were monotonous.

Those of us who had played in previous world championships were able to renew old friendships. I quickly found the Czech goaltender Holecek and the Finn Valtonen. We talked about our experiences and shared news of our families, but not a word about the coming games. It was as if we had come to this beautiful forest to pick mushrooms.

On the following day, we beat the Finns 7-1. Petrov's line was the best on the ice and the local papers wrote: "Kharlamov and Mikhailov defeat the entire Finnish team." The only shot which got past me in this game was accidentally knocked in by our defenseman, Liapkin.

Despite the easy victory, I became worried in the third period. We still had the advantage, but I detected a certain sloppiness and carelessness in our play. Our formations were loose, our shots were tentative. I don't enjoy playing goal at times like this.

My fellow goaltender, Alexander Sidelnikov, also noticed. We room together, so before going to bed, we discussed the problem. We came to the conclusion that our team cools off too soon and that this could cause trouble when we meet stronger teams.

We didn't have to wait long for a test. We were next scheduled to play the decisive game of the championships against Czechoslovakia. Everyone said how strong the Czechs were and that we would have to take this game more seriously, as if we didn't already know that. We had the

"Valeri Kharlamov and Boris Mikhailov defeated the entire Finnish team."

usual light morning practice, then relaxed, but everyone talked only about the importance of beating the Czechs. I think our players were burned out before the game even began.

During the warm-up, I feel great. I stop every shot. All the boys are in good shape.

For some reason we later start very timidly against the Czechs. We cannot organize our attack. Instead they descend upon my cage in full strength. The puck is always at our end of the ice darting around the goal.

I usually don't let such things bother me; I just try to do my job. Now I am getting disturbed. As the game progresses, the tide doesn't turn. "What is going on?" I wonder. The Czechs are skating around at will in our zone. I am getting angry with the defense. We used to have real defensemen—Edward Ivanov, Vitali Davydov, Igor Romischevski and Alexander Ragulin. They weren't afraid to body-check and, if necessary, they would throw themselves in front of shots. Who plays like this now? Maybe one or two?

I holler, "What is going on, you guys?" My mouth is drying up, and my uniform must weigh double from the sweat. I think, "If it keeps on like this, they will kill us." Then I check myself. You can't think like that when you're playing. There has never been a game like this.

Suddenly, a Czech takes the puck away from Alexander Yakushev in our zone. He heads for my cage at full speed. I roll out to meet him, but the puck goes right between my pads. This is the most vulnerable area for any goalie, the area we call the "shed."

There is still no reason to panic. Hold on Vladik. A goalie's courage inspires his teammates and demoralizes the opponents. It's only one goal. Hold on!

A Czech forward shoots for the corner of the net. I move to cover the shot but Tsygankov tries to intercept the puck.

"Between the pads is the most vulnerable area—we call it the 'shed.'"

Instead he deflects it into the far corner. 2-0. "That's something," I say to myself. "This is some game."

A moment later, Petrov gives the puck away to Martinets. I'm screened; I never see the shot. 3-0.

I don't remember when the Czechs have played better than on this evening. Their defense is flawless. Everything works for them. They have a spirit we have lost. What is happening to us?

"We have to pull together," we tell each other between periods. "Get hold of yourselves," our coaches plead.

But when the second period begins, the Czechoslovakian players are again masters of the ice. I have never been so uncomfortable in goal. I am accustomed to being protected by the defense, but here I am being shot at from every direction. One Czech skates through four of our players and passes to Martinets. 6-0. I look at the scoreboard clock and wish for this nightmare to end. When it does, we have lost 7-2.

I had difficulty sleeping that night. I tried reading *The Master and Margarita* by Michael Bulgakov, but I was unable to concentrate. I lay there in the dark, carefully rerunning details of the game.

Defeat bothers me. Perhaps it is because I play for teams which win far more frequently than they lose. Whatever the reason, I experience physical pain after a loss. It's been like that for as long as I can remember. When I played with the children's team and we lost, I could not hold back my tears. I recall one game a year after I received my first hockey uniform. We were playing against the Dynamo team when our goaltender, Alexander Karnaukhov, was injured and had to leave the game. The coach turned to me and said: "Now let's go Vladik, out on the ice!"

I took my place in the crease and was immediately frightened. My fear was just as great as it had been on that 5-meter diving board. When the first shot flew toward our net, I merely closed my eyes and shied away from it. I had 10 goals scored on me that night. After the game, I went to the coach with tears in my eyes and told him that I could never be a goalie.

"Yes, you can," replied Yerfilov, trying to calm me down. "Dry your tears and come to practice tomorrow." I wonder whether he really believed I could become a goalie.

I did not know then that it is impossible to kill fear once and for all, that there are no completely fearless people in the world. The question really is whether a person can suppress his negative emotions—fear, nervousness and apathy. It is necessary to learn to control oneself. You cannot be afraid of the puck. You cannot be afraid of scowling opponents who skate at your cage at a crazy speed. Only one thought has to be in the mind of the goalie: not to let the puck into the goal. Everything else is beside the point. If it hurts—take it. If it is difficult—take it. And think, think all the time how you can play better and more reliably.

When I was twelve, I was seriously hurt for the first time. The puck hit me on the head. The only reason I did not cry was that I was afraid that they would kick me off the team. By that time, hockey was not just a diversion for me. I loved the game with the devotion and passion only a boy can feel. But the day after being hurt, I was like a changed person. In training, I worried about getting hit. I forgot everything I had learned. Again, I had to start from the beginning—again an inner conflict.

Hockey is a rough game. This is especially true for the goaltender. In the final analysis, the force and fury of the opposing team is directed at him. The opposing team is determined to confuse him, to frighten or overwhelm him, to lay him out on the ice—to do anything to put the puck in the net.

A slap shot zooms at the net with the velocity of an artillery shell. The goalie must either catch it with his glove or deflect it—with his stick, his skates, his body, anything at all. The goalie must block that shot.

Other players may make mistakes, but there is no room for an error by the goaltender. When a forward loses the puck, he knows the defense is there to bail him out. When the defense is careless, the goaltender stands ready to correct its mistakes. Only the goalie cannot make a mistake, because his mistakes are goals. He is his own salvation. He must be his own judge.

Ladislav Gorski, a former goaltender for the Czechoslovakian national team, once estimated that a soccer goalie is involved in 10 to 15 plays in an average game. On

"The goalie must block that shot."

the other hand, a hockey goaltender must handle an average of 40 shots per game. There is no time to relax in our game.

Yet, no one has pity for the goaltender. When a shot slips past him into the net, the red light glares like a disaster signal. The fans often boo; even teammates sometimes fail to show their sympathy. No wonder goaltenders have trouble sleeping after a defeat.

We had a team meeting the day after our loss to the Czechs. We all got it from our coaches, particularly the second and third lines. We are rated after each game, and this time the defense got an "F". Boris Mikhailov, usually our most dependable defenseman, said he had never been so nervous; Vyacheslav Anisin, one of our best forwards, became sullen and withdrawn.

I have known Anisin for a long time; we played together on a junior team. He has tremendous enthusiasm for hockey, and I think his best years are still ahead of him. Many think that Anisin is the heir apparent to Valeri Kharlamov. Their styles are remarkably similar. They have a special gift for improvisation and the ability to concentrate on the goal at all times. In these championships, Anisin had not played well; his form had obviously been poor.

"I tried as hard as I could," he confided in me, "but the game just didn't go well."

We watched the game three times on videotape. I relived each goal and tried to examine what went wrong. No one is faultless, and I am satisfied that I played well enough under the circumstances. Even though I rated myself as C-minus for this game, I knew that I would be able to sleep with a clear conscience.

The loss seemed to help us in one way. It brought us together. While many skeptics suggested that we had no chance to win and that our morale and spirit had been broken, we seemed determined to prove them wrong. We appeared to be more serious and better organized. I looked in the faces of my comrades and saw determination to prove that our defeat was an accident. We were resolved to prove we were the strongest team in Helsinki. The skeptics did not know the Soviet national team well enough.

The strength of Soviet hockey goes deeper than the skill of its players. There is our system, the precise teamwork and technical skill which has produced a winning tradition. There is also deep friendship among our players and a high level of consciousness. We have lost hockey games. In sport, no one is insured against defeat. But defeat has never brought dissension to our team; it has only served to bring us closer together. In this respect, we reflect the aims and ideals of the

Soviet people. Every Soviet player must remember that he represents not only himself and his sport but also his country. It is vital to keep this in mind during important games. Millions of fans watch athletes around the world. By our actions, they judge not only us but also our nation and its people.

After the 1972 series against Team Canada, I read the book *Hockey Showdown*, written by Harry Sinden, the coach of the National Hockey League team. Some of Sinden's comments were revealing. He wrote about players who left the Canadian team in Moscow because they weren't getting enough ice time and wanted to return to their clubs' training camps in Canada. It seemed obvious to me these men had no idea of what it means to be a member of a team representing their country.

Sinden points to this when he recounts the players' reaction to the defection of Gilbert Perreault during the 1972 series:

> "The players laughed off Perreault's defection. All the money we made in the exhibition games on this tour is going into a pot to be divided at the end of the tour. When we were coming back to the hotel on the bus after practice today Eddie Johnston voiced the opinion for all to hear: 'Does anyone else want to go home? If we can get rid of a few more the pot will get bigger for the rest of us.' "

The Canadian professionals' principal interest appears to be money.

We were also reminded of this attitude after our first game agains the professionals in Montreal on September 2, 1972. We were shocked when the Canadian team left the ice without exchanging the handshakes which are customary in amateur sport. At first, we were insulted. Later, we discovered that the professionals never salute each other after the final whistle. Phil Esposito, the famous NHL forward, explained to us: "When I've won a game, it means

I've taken money away from the guy I beat. Why would he want to shake my hand?"

The members of the Soviet Union team are taught to think as members of a cohesive unit. Thus we were surprised when we read an excerpt from a Finnish newspaper. In Helsinki, we occasionally visited the Soviet consulate to watch movies or collect our mail. On this morning, an employee of the consulate translated an article which appeared after our loss to the Czechs. I remember it saying approximately this:

> "The Soviet team is doomed because its coaches are occupied with a power struggle. The players have divided their allegiance between two coaches. The partisans of different camps keep away from one another, even at mealtimes. The national team consists of two warring factions."

Hearing this, we begin to laugh. We had never heard such nonsense. I wondered where the correspondents got their information? Had they sucked it out of their thumbs?

April 12. We are matched against the Swedes. Our team is still a bit tight but things are obviously improving. Victory is ours: 3-1. We get another boost when the host Finns upset Czechoslovakia 5-2.

The Finns do not have much time to celebrate. Suddenly, like thunder from a clear sky, it is announced that the Finnish goaltender Vetsel has failed the drug-control test. Victory is given to the Czechs 5-0. It is shocking news. Our players are flabbergasted and we ask each other: What is going on here?

It is not the first incident of doping at these championships. A few days earlier, the Swedish star Ulf Nilsson was disqualified for using Ephedrin. We watch Vetsel as he is interviewed on television. He is practically crying, and he swears that he has not taken Ephedrin in any form.

"I like bananas very much. I also eat candy and chew gum," says Vetsel. "If any of these contain Ephedrin, then I am guilty."

What do I know about doping? Very little. I know there are many drugs which can artificially stimulate the nervous system and produce an unusual burst of energy for a short period of time. Ephedrin is one such substance.

But my teammates and I have always rejected such drugs. We know that any short-term benefits which may be derived from drugs are far outweighed by the dangers of taking drugs. Doping is a terrible poison that eventually attacks the nervous system and other organs. Drugs can make a coward fearless and can transform a weakling into a strong man. But such miracles are temporary—sluggishness, weakness and serious complications inevitably follow.

We have had to play against opponents who were whipped up by stimulants. It is easy to detect them immediately; they are overly-excited and there is a glaze to their eyes. I have been asked many times whether the Canadian professionals are doped. I don't know for sure, but I don't exclude the possibility. There is little interest in controlling doping in the North American leagues.

The developing scandal has made all the players nervous. As we eat our evening meal, someone asks half jokingly, "What if someone spikes our milk with Ephedrin?" Kidding aside, I am not even taking anything for my cold. It is better to stay away from medicine. I have been tested for drugs twice and, of course, the results were negative. Ironically, I was once tested following a game in which I didn't play. It was a game against Poland and I had spent the entire game on the bench, watching Alexander Sidelnikov in goal.

After games and practices in Helsinki, we are besieged by newspapermen. The questions appear to be endless. One reporter asks me: "Mr. Tretyak, if you had an opportunity to begin your hockey career all over again, would you still be a goaltender?"

I don't know whether the reporter is satisfied, because I evade answering him by replying: "I would think about it."

I did play forward once. It was years ago when I played with the Central Army junior team. One of our forwards suddenly fell ill. This happened just before an important game, and there was no one to replace him. The coach asked me to take the forward's position. I scored two goals in two games. I enjoyed being on the other end of a shot, but I would have to think hard before I ever agreed to be a full-time forward.

Playing goal is a very special feeling. They say that a goalie stands in the crease. This is not true—he doesn't stand in the crease, he plays in the crease. He plays! During the entire game, he catches and blocks shots. He performs amazing feats of acrobatics. He is pushed and harassed. While other players change at the end of a shift, the goaltender stays on the ice and never diverts his attention from the puck. He remembers all too well that a goaltender is not permitted to make a mistake. Lev Yashkin, a well-known Soviet soccer goalie, once declared that in any sport there is no position as noble as that of goaltender. I would like to add that there is no position more difficult.

Speed, dexterity, strength, endurance, faultless coordination—all these qualities are indispensable to a goalie. People often ask me why a goaltender needs strength, and I remind them that a goaltender must perform his duties while wearing equipment which weighs 15 to 20 kilograms (33 to 44 pounds). A goaltender also needs sharp eyes, intuition, courage, a strong will, a keen sense of balance and the ability to orient himself instantly.

The goaltender must also be able to deal with the pressure of this lightning-fast game. There have been games where I have touched the puck only twice, but the tension has been so great that I was barely able to drag my feet at the

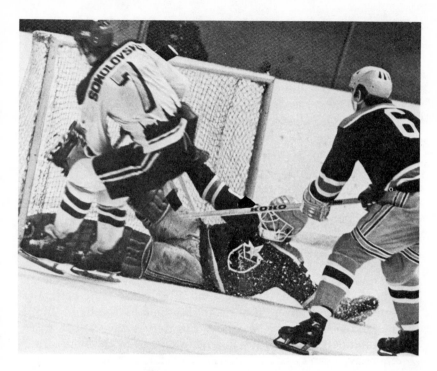

"Speed, dexterity, strength, endurance, faultless coordination—there is no position more difficult."

intermission. Jacques Plante, the famous Canadian goaltender, once gave me a copy of his book, *Goaltending*. He wrote on it:

> "I believe that you will be glad to have this book since we became friends during your last visit to Canada. You are one of the best young goalies that ever visited us. I hope that you will play for many years and will become the best goalie in the world."

I read Plante's book with a great deal of pleasure. I was particularly interested in his comments on the pressure facing a goaltender.

"Pressure is the name of the game," he writes. "The stronger the team he plays against, the more pressure the goalie feels—the kind of tension that produces ulcers and has forced some great goalies to quit the game—goalies like Wilf Cude, Frank McCool, Bill Durnan, Gerry McNeil.

"Roger Crozier said, 'There is no way people will understand our particular kind of pressure. Anyone who isn't a goaltender probably won't experience once what we experience hundreds of times; even the players don't know what the goalie goes through in a game.'

"Wilf Cude once told me when I visited him in Rouen, Quebec, that one day he was so tense, thinking of the game he had to play that night, that he threw his steak at his wife. After it hit the wall, he couldn't believe what he had done, and not long after that, he decided he had had enough of this life and retired . . . .

"And how about 'Mister Goalie,' Glenn Hall? I can still see him on game night, deathly ill, burping, swallowing hard, and holding a towel in front of his mouth, just in case he couldn't make it in time to the bathroom. His nerves were so bad that he often left the ice in the middle of a game to throw up. To this day, I can't understand how he lasted so long and played so well under these conditions."

Not all goaltenders develop ulcers or become ill before a game. But in general, Plante paints an accurate picture of the tension facing a goaltender. And yet, he also says, "I still think playing goal is the best position in hockey."

When someone asks if I would rather be a forward or a goaltender, I find it a difficult question to answer. But after weighing the pros and cons of being a goalie, I have to agree with Plante—there is no other position I would rather play.

April 18. We would be playing our most important game in this tournament, the second game against the Czechoslovakian national team. It was a game we had to win.

We warmed up by crushing Poland 17-0. That victory was more than convincing but even after the game we weren't

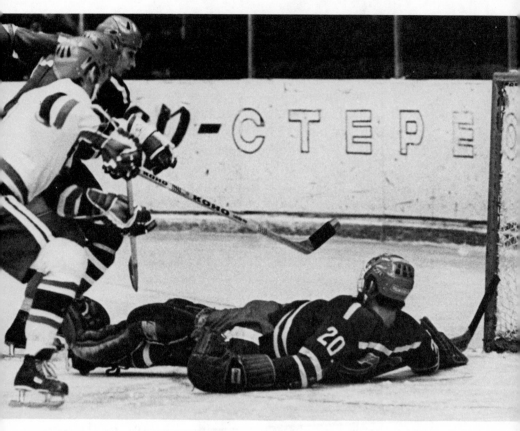

"Not all goaltenders develop ulcers. I have to agree with Plante–there is no other position I would rather play."

completely satisfied. At times, we were perfectly coordinated but then we would suddenly fall apart. The defense would forget its responsibilities and rush forward with breakneck speed. The forward lines wouldn't pass the puck. In short, we didn't play well, regardless of the one-sided score. It was a poor dress rehearsal for the showdown against the Czechs.

Our coaches made several line changes before the Czech game. Vladimir Petrov was hurt, and Alexander Maltsev took his place on the first line. Yuri Lebedev replaced Maltsev on the second line. Many of us were surprised by these bold changes, but as the game wore on they proved to be good moves.

The game begins. I look directly down the ice and see the Czech goalie Holecek. I can't see his face behind the mask, but by the way he is shifting from one foot to the other I know that he is very tense. Holecek is a great goalie. He is much older than I and knows all the fine points of our trade. It is almost impossible to beat him on a shot from close in. He has phenomenal reflexes, is courageous and calculating. Holecek has only one weakness—when he misses a shot, he has a tendency to tighten up and make mistakes. The secret is to put pressure on Holecek so that he makes a mistake early in the game.

Holecek does not make the first mistake. I do. Tsygankov is given a 5-minute penalty in the first period, and the Czechs score on the power play. As I fish the puck out of the net, I glance at the penalty box. There is a look of shame and disgust in Tsygankov's face; he knows he has let his team down.

Yakushev evens the score after a prolonged siege in the second period. We have many scoring chances, but Holecek is brilliant until Yakushev bangs in a rebound. As I expected, Holecek becomes tense. He soon makes another mistake and Maltsev puts us ahead 2-1.

Yet the Czechs haven't quit. They won't beat me again in this game but it takes great effort to stop them. Martinets, Stchastny and the others keep the pressure on and send me scrambling from one goalpost to another in a mad dance. Their shots are strong and precise. It is impossible to explain how I stop them.

A Czech player has the puck and is racing toward our zone. He is still far away, but I know he can shoot from anywhere, and I am already 98 percent tuned in. A split second later, my entire attention is focused on his moves.

Yakushev evens the score.

"I look straight into his eyes. If he returns the stare, it means he will shoot."

When he shoots, I am able to cover the shot and deflect it with my pads.

Now it is Stchastny with the puck. He is an extremely dangerous player, whether he is shooting or setting up a teammate with a pass. But I have learned that Stchastny has a small weakness—his eyes betray his intentions. I look straight into his eyes. If he returns the stare, it means he will shoot. More often, he will turn his eyes to the right and look for Martinets. That's how it is now, the pass is on Martinets's stick. Here's the shot. Hold on, Tretyak!

Between the second and third periods, the sweat rolls down my back in buckets. This is surprising because, unlike my teammates, I never drink water during a game. I'm breathing heavily, and I'm sure that I look pitiful.

Boris Kulagin, one of our coaches, comes to me and says, "Hold on, Vladik." Then he says unexpectedly, "Do you remember how you used to do 20 laps around the rink?"

Indeed, I do remember, and I smile at Kulagin. He has reminded me of my first year with the Central Army junior

Coach Boris Kulagin: "Hold on, Vladik."

team. Kulagin was the coach and he made each of us skate 20 times around the ice. The other boys were as much as four years older than I and were accustomed to such exercise. As they skated without difficulty, I tired quickly. After 10 laps, I stopped. I was exhausted and thought I would die.

"Have pity on Vladik, he is still young," my teammates implored.

But Kulagin answered, "If Tretyak can take this, he will be a good hockey player." Somehow, I managed to finish. It seems that Kulagin never forgot that episode.

I smile again, without reason, and get up to resume my position on the ice. The intermission is over.

We won the game 3-1. Analyzing the game later we realized we had won, not only because we played better but also because we were more daring than our opponents. Our team play was sharp. Our preparations for this game were very serious. Before the game, I stood in the dressing room and told myself, "You must play well. You must. You simply have no right to let up in this game."

Our final game in the 1974 world championships was against Sweden. The Swedes are renowned for their fine defensive play. We decided to attack continuously and to break down their defenses at any cost. When the game was over, we were the winners 3-1.

The score might have been higher but their goaltender, Christer Abrahamsson, performed miracles. Generally, his play is uneven—sometimes brilliant, sometimes mediocre. Abrahamsson is at his best in a close game, and against the Soviets he did not budge.

Even when Mikhailov shot from point-blank range, the Swedish goalie held his ground. Abrahamsson is an interesting character. He is a curly-haired, good-natured fellow off the ice, and I've always wondered where his good nature goes during a game. Christer is like a fighting cock—you just touch him and he starts hollering and swinging his stick. In my opinion, a goalie should contain his emotions deep inside. It is of no use to be hot-headed.

The Swedish team reminds me of the Canadian professionals. The players are fast, energetic and offensive-minded. It is not surprising that several North American teams have begun recruiting the Swedish stars.* Swedish hockey also has a great tradition of developing

*Both Thommy and Christer Abrahamsson now play for the New England Whalers.

"Anatoli Firsov has one of the most powerful shots in hockey."

outstanding goaltenders. As far as I know, Swedish
goaltenders are only afraid of one man, our own Anatoli
Firsov. Firsov has one of the most powerful shots in hockey.
I am lucky he is playing for our team and that I have never
had to face his shot. I know that some goalies have seen him
wind up and surrendered by closing their eyes before he
shoots.

After the victory over the Swedes, we returned to our
hotel room. I accompanied Repnev and Lebedev to their
room, and we were soon joined by Sidelnikov, Anisin and
Kapustin. We decided to have a glass of champagne before
the official reception. After one sip, I felt nauseous and had

to leave the room in a hurry.The monstrous tension of the past few days had caught up with me.

Later, we returned to the Yahalli Sports Palace for the colorful closing ceremonies. Our captain, Boris Mikhailov, stepped forward to receive two silver cups; the rest of us were presented with flowers.

Then, it was off to the Finland Concert Hall for the reception. John (Bunny) Ahearne, the president of the International Ice Hockey Federation, appeared on the dais and delivered a long speech. Strangely, he barely mentioned our team, the world champions. Obviously, his sympathy lay with the others, and he could not hide this fact.

There were more awards. I was acknowledged the best goalie at the world championships. It was like a dream come true. I have always wanted to be the best—first on my club team, then in the European league championships, and finally, with the Soviet national team. Some may regard this as vanity. But at no time has my drive to be the best detracted from the interests of the team. To the contrary, I have always placed the welfare of my team above any personal goals.

The fact that I have been named as the best goaltender in the world championships is to the credit of my teammates, my coaches and most of all, my first teacher, Antoli Tarasov. To this day, only one other Soviet has been named the all-star goalie in the world championships. That was Nikolai Puchkov in the 1959 world competition in Prague. He is currently training the Leningrad team of the Sports Club of the Army. Before he became keen on hockey he tended goal for the Air Force soccer team in Moscow.

This day was the happiest of my life. We were champions of the world. I was the best goalie. No one dared ask if I would exchange my career guarding the cage for something else.

"Like a dream come true–I have always wanted to be the best, on my club team, in the European league, finally with the Soviet national team."

We return home by rail, touching Soviet soil first at Vyborg where the station platform again overflows with fans. People congratulate us. We are touched to the depths of our souls.

"Thank you, thank you," my teammates repeat again and again.

I think: "How could we have possibly lost?"

May 1974

I still can't come to my senses after the world championships, yet there are so many important things to occupy my time and thoughts. For example, there was the national championship series. Our Central Army has built a winning tradition over many years but this year, we were relegated to second place behind the Soviet Wings. Then, there is school—another year has begun at the university. My son Dimka is exactly one year old and has taken his first steps by himself. There is so much news.

Among all these events, there is something special, something I will always remember with excitement. The Moscow city organization has selected me to participate in the seventeenth convention of the Communist Youth League, the Komsomol. The Komsomol meets once every four years in the Kremlin, and it is the greatest honor for a young person to be selected as a delegate. Recently, I have served as the Komsomol organizer for our hockey team. It was in this capacity that I attended the convention of the Moscow city organization where I was selected for the national convention. I had told my comrades in Moscow of my work with the hockey team and had assured them we would win the world championship.

Many people ask me about the role of a Komsomol organizer on a hockey team. In our club, as in most other

Valdislav Tretyak with his son Dimka.

Soviet hockey clubs, almost every player is a member of the Komsomol or of the Communist Party. The primary task of the Komsomol organization is the ideological and political education of the team members. We have regular meetings, publish a newsletter and organize lectures and meetings with celebrated Soviet citizens—cosmonauts, writers, actors and scientists. We salute the accomplishments of our fellow Komsomol members.

Many of our hockey players are students or college graduates. The majority of the students attend the Institute of Physical Culture. Some, like Kovalev, attend the Highway Institute or the Technical University of Moscow, Romishevski's alma mater. The Komsomol office helps arrange training and keeps an eye on its members to see that no one falls behind or violates training rules. There is plenty to do.

I arrived at the Kremlin on April 23, 1974, wearing my parade officer's uniform. As I took my place in the fifteenth row of the convention palace, I was surrounded by outstanding young men and women. Many had medals and awards for their achievements, and I recognized some from newspaper photographs and television. There were workers and collective farmers, cosmonauts and warriors, high schoolers and college students, scientists and actors—the finest representatives of Soviet youth were there.

I recognized some famous sports figures sitting in an area not far from where I was seated. There were Ludmilla Turischeva, the Olympic gold medallist in gymnastics; the figure skater Irena Rodnina, track star Valeri Borzov and Vladimir Vasin, an outstanding diver. My heart was drowning in a wave of pride. I, Vladislav Tretyak, had been entrusted to represent Soviet hockey at this convention—I was representing a team which had won the world championship 13 times.

In the following two days, there were many happy moments. I signed at least a thousand autographs, answered hundreds of questions and received many congratulations on behalf of my teammates and our glorious hockey organization. Without that organization, none of this would have been possible.

I also had the opportunity to meet the famous soccer goalie, Lev Yashin, on April 25. I had idolized Yashin as a boy, and now I was talking with him in one of the hallways of the convention palace. It was easy to understand why this man is the pride of Soviet soccer, a fine sportsman who received tributes from most of the world's best players in his farewell game.

Then came the most important moment of my life: my address from the podium of the convention. Never, not even in the most important games, have I been as excited as I was on that podium. I had been entrusted to represent all Soviet sportsmen and, specifically, my teammates on the Soviet national team.

"My comrades of the national hockey team, who have won the European and world titles for the thirteenth time, asked me to report," I told the convention, "and tell this gathering that the Komsomol assignment has been fulfilled."

During the convention, I often thought of the veteran Soviet stars whose tradition we carry forward today. I was helped to the top by such world-renowned players as Victor Konovalenko, Anatoli Firsov and Alexander Ragulin. When I first began skating, these players were at the peak of their careers. Thousands of boys dreamed of receiving their autographs, but I had been selected to train with them and observe their styles which became classical. My examples were the imperturbable and unbeatable Konovalenko, the brilliant forward Firsov and the reliable defenseman Ragulin.

These champions never looked down on newcomers. Konovalenko, who was twice my age, had patiently revealed to me the secrets of the goaltender's art. He had taught me

"I had been entrusted to represent Soviet hockey at the national Komsomol congress."

not to get excited and to control myself. The record speaks for itself—he played on seven world championship teams and was an Olympic gold medallist! What other goalie can boast of such titles?

Legends grew up about Konovalenko's modesty. Quiet, even somewhat dour in appearance, Victor seemed determined to make others unaware of his presence. But

"Victor Konovalenko had fantastic intuition; it often seemed as if pucks flew into his glove by themselves—but he never lost his cool."

when a game began, Victor would take his place in the crease and become transformed. Apathy would be replaced by lightning reactions and daring. He had fantastic intuition, and it often seemed as if pucks flew into his glove by themselves. He had one quality which was most important—he never lost his cool.

I don't remember any player on the Soviet national team who commanded more respect than Konovalenko. They respected his devotion to his home city of Gorki. Victor played his entire career with the Torpedo club in Gorki, even though he had had more enticing offers to play elsewhere. He was respected for his sense of fair play, his devotion to hockey, for his valor and steadfastness. He was a brilliant successor to the outstanding Soviet goaltenders, Puchkov and Mkrtychan.

I first participated in the world championships in 1970 when Konovalenko was our first-string goaltender. He played marvelously. Without hesitation, I would have selected him as the outstanding goalie in the series. I particularly remember one episode against the Swedes. It was late in the second period and we were losing 2-1. A Swedish player had a break, but he shot too soon and Victor was able to throw himself down in a desperate attempt to block the puck. As Victor hit the ice, the Swede was unable to stop. His skate cut Konavalenko in the face. Victor was rushed to the hospital; I took over in goal. I allowed two easy shots to beat me and we lost the game 4-2.

That loss put a great deal of pressure on us the following day. It was our last game, and we had to win it to be world champions. If we lost, we would finish third. I remember the stands bursting with applause when Victor Konovalenko appeared on the ice. He took his place in the crease and, of course, we won.

That was the first time I experienced the joy of a great victory. It is impossible to describe the feelings that fill the heart of a sportsman when his country's flag is raised and the anthem is played in his honor.

On our return from the 1970 world championships, we were met by hundreds of people at the Moscow Airport. Relatives, friends and hockey fans greeted us on all sides. Only Victor remained alone for some time. All of his friends and relatives were home in Gorki.

I was approached by a reporter from a radio station. "Congratulations, Vladislav," he said.

"Thank you," I replied.

"Tell me, what did you feel when you became a world champion?"

"I have never been so happy in my whole life."

"What lessons did you learn in Stockholm?"

"Lessons? I think I learned the value of real courage," I replied, looking around for Victor. "Victor," I shouted, "may I say something about you in this interview?"

And then there is Anatoli Firsov! He is one of the most brilliant skaters in the history of Soviet hockey. What a pity he never had the opportunity to meet the Canadian professionals on the ice. It would have been a marvelous duel—Anatoli Firsov against Phil Esposito.

Firsov could not be held back. Whenever he went onto the ice, the stands would hum with excitement in anticipation of a goal. As I have said earlier, Firsov's shot struck fear in opposing goaltenders. He shot quickly, without any preparation, but the puck flew with such velocity that it was impossible to follow. We particularly valued Anatoli for his ability to lead the team in difficult moments, to unite the line. He was the captain of the Central Army Sports Club team and its playing coach. He has now retired as a player but remains with us as coach of the army team.

Firsov's name is tied to the 10-year history of children's competition organized by the Golden Puck club. Anatoli is

The national Golden Puck championships are held in March during the school holidays. Medals are awarded, and the outstanding players appear on television.

one of the founders of this club, as well as one of its most active members.

The Golden Puck competition is held each year and involves almost three million boys on tens of thousands of teams. The teams are created in schools, neighborhoods and small counties. The coaches are drawn from the communities and include workers, students and military men. The competition goes on throughout the winter, first on the community level and then in series to determine city and provincial champions. The winners on these levels qualify for the National Golden Puck championships.

The national championships are held in March during the school holidays. The best sports palaces are reserved for these youngsters; leading referees officiate. Medals are bestowed on the championship teams, and the outstanding players appear on television. Many players and coaches attend these championship games and assist in the development of these young players. Men like Arkadi Tchernyshev, Vladimir Yurzinov, Vyatcheslav Starshinov, Vitali Davydov, Igor Romishevski and Victor Kuzkin, even Anatoli Firsov, train the boys and teach them the basics.

The president of the club is a man of great authority: Meritorious Master of Sport and Meritorious Coach of the USSR, Anatoli Tarasov. The central committee also includes responsible Komsomol and sports workers, coaches, managers of companies that produce hockey equipment and outstanding sportscasters.

The Golden Puck competition has already produced quite a few good hockey players, but more importantly, it produces strong men. Boys who participate in hockey learn valuable lessons which can help them in other fields. They learn nobility and chivalry, tenaciousness and courage. It is no accident that one of our popular songs says, "Cowards do not play hockey."

Alexander Ragulin played on 10 world championship teams and was the most reliable defenseman in hockey. Ragulin could be depended upon in any circumstances, an advantage for the goaltender behind his powerful back.

I particularly remember a game against Leningrad. It was, as they say, a run-of-the-mill game with no particular significance. One of the Leningrad players fired a hard shot at our net, and I knew at once it would go by me. Only Ragulin was in position to stop the shot, but he could only do it by placing his face in the path of the puck. He did it without hesitation.

Ragulin was a well-balanced and gentle giant, a favorite of the whole team. He worked hard and was always giving advice to rookies. In my opinion, he was the ideal defenseman.

It has been established that hockey originated in Canada. The first recorded game was played in 1879. The Canadians themselves say that hockey is an important part of their lives, and after many visits to the Land of the Maple Leaf, I am prepared to agree with this statement.

I have been told that Canadian children learn to skate before they learn to walk and that four-year-old children know how to carry a puck and shoot it. However, hockey has long since ceased to be a Canadian monopoly. This fast-moving and daring game fits into our dynamic century. Hockey has spread rapidly throughout the world. In the Soviet Union, it has millions of adherents and is undoubtedly the number-one game. A journalist friend, who has been to the North Pole, says that crews on the floating ice camps start playing hockey as soon as the polar night sets in. There is more than enough ice under their feet.

I get letters from youngsters in Georgia and Uzbekistan where there is no winter and it is impossible to make a rink.

"Alexander Ragulin, a well-balanced and gentle giant, a favorite of the whole team—in my opinion he was the ideal defenseman."

Nevertheless, these youngsters tell me that they play hockey on the pavement without skates.

Recently, the Soviet national team was invited to the Star City by the cosmonauts. We told them about our experiences at the world championships and answered their questions. It turns out that the cosmonauts are not only rabid hockey fans but also like to skate themselves.

One of the cosmonauts, Anatoli Filipchenko showed me a scar under his right eye. "Got it from hockey," he explained.

Another cosmonaut, Pavel Popovitch came to me and said, "Let's get acquainted, colleague. I am also a goalie, on our Cosmic team."

Alexi Leonov, one of the directors of the space program, told us how he once chided the cosmonauts while they were in orbit. According to the schedule, they should have been sleeping. Instead, they were listening to hockey on the radio.

But it is time to return from the cosmic orbit. I have to get back to the books. I have an examination session coming up in May at the Institute of Physical Culture and I must study—educational techniques, physiology, psychology, social sciences.

It is true that I can't imagine my life without hockey, but I have many other interests. Sports help a person learn and grow, but they should not destory his interests in other areas. Here at the Central Army Sports Club, everyone studies—some at universities, others at technical schools. Our coaches are constantly reminding us: "First of all, you have to learn to be real people, then you can learn to be hockey players."

What does the phrase "real people" mean? I understand it like this: honest, educated, with principles and a firm position in life. A hockey player will never become a good craftsman if he does not develop in himself goals and self-discipline, a need to continuously expand his horizons. If a person ceases to develop intellectually, if his curiosity is dulled and the circle of his interests diminishes to the size of a puck, then inevitably his mastery of the sport will also cease to grow. The practice of any sport, including hockey, is a creative exercise. Creativity is only for the curious.

Of course, it isn't easy to combine hockey with studies. We are always travelling. Games, training, rallies. There is very little time left to study. One gets so tired that often one does not feel like picking up a book. However, there is a compensation. Sport teaches us to value each and every minute. We learn to set up goals and how to reach them.

Igor Romishevski, who recently finished his playing career with our club, successfully defended his thesis for the degree of Doctor of Science and is now a department chairman at the Moscow Institute of Physics and Technology. Another famous Soviet hockey player, Vyacheslav Starshinov, is preparing to defend his thesis in education, and Vladimir Yurzinov is a graduate of the school of journalism at Moscow University.

The Canadians describe Soviet hockey as precise, intellectual. Yes, compared with the uncontestably courageous, highly technical but somewhat straight-forward play of the Canadian professionals, the actions of Soviet hockey players are more flexible and more thoughtful. Why is that so? Perhaps, it is because hockey is a business for the Canadians. It is their livelihood. There is a saying: Any specialist is like a stream and knows only one course. I may be oversimplifying it, but could this be the cause of the unimaginative Canadian style?

In one of my courses at the Institute, a psychologist asked me a series of questions concerning the psychological aspects of sports education. Our discussion was recorded. Following are excerpts from that interview:

> *Psychologist:* Let us start with preparations for a game. How do you, as a goaltender, prepare for a game?
> *Tretyak:* My preparations differ from those of the other members of the team. I have to prepare myself for the entire 60 minutes of a game. Goalies, unlike the other players, do not have an opportunity to rest. Therefore, it is very important to retain the maximum emotional energy for the game. This is one of my most important rules in regard to my psychological make-up.
> How does one preserve energy? As a rule, I sleep before a game. No matter what is happening, no matter how important

the game is going to be, I force myself to sleep. I know that if I do not sleep, I will be less attentive on the ice and will tire more quickly.

P: How do you manage to maintain concentration for such a lengthy period?

T: Aside from various technical exercises, I use self-hypnosis to psyche myself up for the game. Before the game, I tell myself: "You must stand up well, you must not let the puck through." During the game, depending upon the situation, I tell myself, "More attention, don't be distracted. Now you may rest, relax your shoulder muscles. Pay attention to your face, don't wrinkle your brow, make it smooth." I feel at ease, fresh, I breathe deeply. I take the same trouble to prepare myself for any game, no matter who the opponents are.

P: In the championship games against Czechoslovakia, you allowed 6 goals.

T: Actually, it was 7. I could have allowed 15. I thought about it for a long time, asking myself why did this happen? My conclusion was that I did not prepare myself properly for this game. Before the game, the coaches and reporters were telling us that we had only one game in the championships, the game against Czechslovakia, and that we must win it. The Czechs and only the Czechs! They simply frightened us before the game. We call it "pumping up," and we lost before we even got on the ice. I was also disoriented. Fear triumphed over our self-assurance. We all began making mistakes from the very beginning, and the goals poured in.

My approach is to rest when the puck is in the opponent's end and is being controlled by my teammates. I am calm. My muscles are relaxed. I can't be tense to the limit all the time. In the game against Czechoslovakia, our players were losing the puck in our end continuously. In a situation such as that, I was unable to relax and call upon my reserve strength.

P: What do you understand by the term "fast recovery"? Is your consciousness directed toward yourself or do you follow the tactics of the offense?

T: I think it's very important to get hold of yourself after giving up a goal or two. These are noticeable psychological blows. I force myself not to think about why a goal was scored—that will come later when I analyze the videotape of the game. I simply pull myself together quickly and convince myself that nothing has happened, that I am

"I use self-hypnosis to psych myself up for the game. I tell myself, don't be distracted, relax your shoulder muscles, breathe deeply."

"I always try to follow the threads of the game, to analyze the play."

doing well. A goalie has to continually prepare himself for the next shot. He has a very responsible position. Occasionally, when we lead by quite a few goals, the forwards may allow themselves an opportunity to relax, perhaps even make a few bad passes. A goalie doesn't have this leeway.

I always try to follow the threads of a game. I attempt to analyze the play of my teammates—this one played well, this one poorly. That one should have passed to his wing on the last rush. I try to continuously follow the pattern of the game.

P: What thoughts do you have when the lines are rotated? How does this affect your emotions?

T: Changing players naturally affects the mood of the game. When our first line is on the ice, I am calm and confident. But when the rookies come out, I am afraid that they may make mistakes. I try to prompt them and encourage them, and naturally I am more tense.

P: Does that mean you adjust your thoughts and try to make yourself more alert when these players are on the ice?

T: Yes.

P: Does your prompting disturb the other players?

T: I don't think so. Of course, when someone makes a mistake, I try to avoid insulting words. I believe it's better to encourage a player, especially after he has made a mistake.

P: That is true. We are talking about the tension of the game, in other words, a stress situation. In such a situation, a word not only carries its literal meaning but also an emotional impact which can hurt a person very deeply. I think that this is one of the causes of nervous breakdowns in any type of human endeavour connected with a high level of tension or responsibility. Athletes are subject to a chain reaction of negative emotions. You correctly stated that a team can't be "pumped up" and aimed only at victory. That pressure results when the sports management feels more for itself than for the team.

T: Yes, in this sense, I feel a great deal depends on the goalie. The most important thing, however, is not what you say to your comrades but how you play. If a team is weak but the goaltender plays brilliantly, this can inspire his teammates and demoralize the opposition. When a goalie demonstrates reliability, the defense can move forward and initiate the attack without fear. The goalkeeper instills confidence in a team like no other player can.

P: I am interested in your concept of time while you are on the ice. For example, how do you feel when there are three seconds remaining in a game?

T: Well, we were ahead in a decisive game of the world championships in Finland, and there were only three seconds left until the final whistle. You can literally feel that time; it fills you with expectation. Soon the whistle is going to blow and you will be a champion! This expectation can be felt even more sharply than the end result. Sometimes time rushes by on the ice; sometimes it is just the opposite. But you can never forget the clock. We have had some sad examples of a loss of the sense of time. For example, in the final game of the series against the NHL All-Stars in Moscow, we lost in the final 15 seconds. We relaxed and we paid for it. It was a good lesson. From that moment on, I have not permitted myself to relax until the very end of a contest. The lesson is remembered.

P: Do you try to visualize a game beforehand in your imagination? If so, are there specific variants for each team?

T: I can tell you how I train the morning of a game, and that may provide you with an example of what you're talking about. After a brief warmup, I immediately concentrate on details. For example, I think of various possible shots and how to best deflect them. I imagine the opponents' moves and select the best position for each situation.

When I do this, I visualize the opponents not as abstractions but as they appear in real life. If we are going to play the Canadians, I run the Canadian players and their various formations through my mind. If we are to play the Swedes, I think about the Swedes, and so on.

P: Let us assume you have replaced an injured teammate during a game. It is an extreme situation and the adjustment time is very short. How do you cope with this situation?

T: I warm up instantaneously. I try to mobilize myself through words. I tell myself, "This will be difficult . . . get ready." The fact that I have been in the rink and following

"After a brief warmup, I immediately concentrate on details. I think of various possible shots and visualize the opponents' moves."

the action helps in that situation because I know what has been happening.

P: Let us now assume an impossible situation. Suppose that you were sitting on the bench before replacing a teammate but you were blindfolded. Would this absence of a visual evaluation of the game affect your actions?

T: Definitely, my actions would be affected, but I'm not sure whether this would be a good thing or a bad thing. When I look at the rink, I can't help but become involved. Occasionally, the tension of watching my teammates is so great that I tire more than if I were in goal. I can't say definitely which is better—to watch the game in order to be a part of the action or not to watch it in an attempt to conserve my emotional energy.

P: How important is it to know the strengths and weakness of an opponent?

T: It is very important. As a goalie, I must be familiar with the playing styles, the strengths and weaknesses of all the players our team may meet on the ice. I am occasionally asked whether I'm afraid of one player or another. I'm not afraid of anybody. However, I try to make a detailed study of each opponent and plan my tactics accordingly. I know how each player will try to get around me, which players will force me out of the crease to cut down the angle of a shot and which players I can only meet head-on from the cage.

P: How would you describe your temperament? Are you excitable or calm? In other words, do you hide your inner stresses or do you react to each situation quickly, adapting to the changing conditions?

T: That is a difficult question for me to answer definitely. It appears that you must arrive at your own conclusion from observing my play.

P: The psychologist Pavlov divided people into two basic types, the artistic and the contemplative. Which type would you classify yourself; are you dominated by a rational approach or are you governed by emotions?

T: It seems that I am more on the rational side.

P: Three motives can be identified in any activity: the desire to obtain an end result, satisfaction with the activity itself and the desire for social approval. Which one of these motives do you consider most important for you at this time?

T: I believe it is the first. The purpose of a great sportsman is to become a champion, to be the best. Otherwise, it would be simply an exercise.

P: You mentioned some time ago that when your parents took you to hockey school you were indifferent to the game and its results. You were most impressed by the external benefits, the uniform, for example. It seems evident that your motives have changed. Do you derive pleasure from the activity itself or do you consider hockey work?

T: I think it's work. I can even say that all major sports are very intensive work.

P: Do you experience any aesthetic pleasure from your activities on the ice?

T: Yes. Occasionally, I block a puck which is "labelled" as we say. It should be a goal, but I stop it and I actually get goose pimples. I blocked it! It is an indescribable feeling. But I want to note that I feel bad when this happens. I think it is a bad thing when a person admires himself all the time.

Tretyak is forced out of the crease to cut down the angle of a shot.

P: How do you feel during a game? Do you have an opportunity for reflection; do you ever see yourself from outside as though someone else were in the goal instead of you?

T: At the beginning of the game, I can make a good stop, and that's all I need to acquire the necessary self-confidence. I tell myself, "Everything is normal. No need to worry. You'll manage." However, there is a danger. Complete self-confidence borders on relaxation. It is very important not to lower one's emotional involvement. I could never take myself out of the action, because that would detract from my concentration and attention. One has to find a "golden mean."

P: Are you weakened or strengthened by a mishap early in the game?

T: If a goal is scored against me at the beginning of the game, it is much more difficult to recover my confidence—much more difficult than if the goal were scored, for example, at the twentieth minute. An early goal creates significant psychological trauma. The attackers know this, and they'll go all out to score early. They feel out the goalie. What is being asked of the goalie at that moment? The most important thing

"Occasionally I block a puck which is 'labelled.' It should be a goal, but I stop it—I actually get goose pimples, an indescribable feeling."

is not to lose confidence in his ability. He mustn't think about the possibility of surrendering an early goal. The greatest goaltenders are the ones who, even after giving up a goal, can find the strength to continue playing as if nothing has happened.

P: You play with a mask. Does it narrow your field of vision?

T: I don't notice this. I'm so accustomed to the mask that it doesn't bother me at all. I could even walk down the street wearing the mask and I would feel quite comfortable.

P: Can you tell us anything about the specific reflex sensations of a goalie?

T: A goalie has many reflexes but they're all based on one stimulus—don't let the puck in the net. Even if a goalie accidentally takes his glove off and the puck is shot at the same moment, he'll attempt to catch it with his bare hand. That's a reflex. It is an unconscious motion, but it is strongly rooted in the conscious, as if it were controlled by some deep-seated mechanism in the brain. Occasionally, the puck is shot at full force from a distance of 15 feet. No conscious action or simple reaction can help here. One needs a reaction that has been perfected earlier and the arm automatically goes up to block the puck. If one had to think how to block it and with what, it would be hopelessly late. By the time one makes such a decision, the red light would be glowing behind his back as a signal of disaster.

Why did I pick the Institute of Physical Culture for my education? The answer is simple—in the future, I want to become a coach or a sports organizer.

I'm deeply convinced of the great importance of physical fitness in the lives of our generation and of those to follow us. The Soviet scientist A. Berg calculated that, as recently as 100 years ago, man had to perform 96 percent of all his work. Now we have shifted a large part of this burden onto the shoulders of machines. This means our bodies have to compensate for the lack of physical activity. The best compensation is sport. Sports improve creativity, heighten ability to work and aid in the development of such valuable attributes as sharpness of the mind, curiosity, vigor and reaction time. Can any of these be harmful?

Incidentally, I am disturbed by the fact many people do not recognize the need for physical fitness. The phenomenal records of Olympic champions correspond to the progress of science, culture and technology. But there is a wide discrepancy between the physical perfection of the Olympic record holders (who are basically a small group of young people) and the physical state of the general public. For too many people physical fitness has not become a real need. Many people regard it as of secondary importance. That is a

"A goalie needs reactions that have been perfected earlier. If one had to think how to block the puck and with what, it would be hopelessly late."

pity. The scientists give us a frightening warning—the heart begins to deteriorate as early as age 13 without proper exertion.

A human being has to be strong! Sooner or later, every person is called upon to demonstrate determination, willpower and endurance. But even if one does not have to endure any particular hardship, can it be bad to be always strong and vigorous? The harmonious development of the personality is unthinkable without active participation in physical activity.

I'm preparing myself for serious work in the area of sport. In studying history, education and philosophy, I am more convinced of the great power of physical fitness. The Greek philosopher Plato said that a person is lame if he can't write or can't swim. Pythagoras was regarded as a champion boxer. The father of medicine, Hippocrates, was an excellent wrestler and horseback rider. The 80-year-old king of Sparta,

Agesilaus, not only commanded his troops on the battlefield but also played an active role in the fighting.

Here are some equally impressive examples from more recent times. The famous Russian poet, Alexander Pushkin, took lessons in boxing, practiced shooting and bathed in icy waters each winter. The English poet, Byron, swam the Dardanelles. The world famous Norwegian polar explorer, Fridtjof Nansen, won his country's cross-country skiing championship 12 times. The Danish physicist Neils Bohr, the American writer Ernest Hemingway and the French physicist Frederic Joliot Curie were among the many other notable people occupied with sports.

The mission of sport is one of the most noble on earth. Man wants to be strong and beautiful, quick and courageous, dexterous and enduring. I wish to dedicate my life to helping him in this task.

August 1974

My vacation flew by so quickly that I wondered if I had actually had one. My wife Tatyana and I relaxed at the Golden Sands in Bulgaria, but too soon it was time to return to Moscow and begin training for another season. We began in early July and it seemed I went from standing still to a full gallop.

We never before worked as hard as we did this summer. One of our new coaches, former Soviet hockey star Konstantin Loktev, decided that I should train with the same intensity as the other players. That meant that in addition to my specific goalie exercises I joined the other players in running cross-country, lifting weights and passing special fitness tests.

Anatoli Tarasov and Arcady Chernishev coached the Soviet national team until the spring of 1972, when they asked permission to retire due to their ages. Vsevolod Bobrov and Boris Kulagin took over, but after our disappointing second place in the world competition in Prague, Kulagin was named Senior Coach. He currently has two assistants, Loktev and Vladimir Ursinov, both previously popular hockey stars on the national team. Loktev is also senior hockey coach of the Central Army Sports Club, and Ursinov holds the same rank for the Moscow team Dynamo.

National coaches Anatoli Tarasov and Arcady Chernishev.

Loktev, looking ahead to the coming season, predicted it would be difficult and wanted me to be well-prepared. In July, we practiced three times a day—an hour before breakfast; two hours after breakfast and another two hours in the evening. An outsider could have become tired just watching us go through our routine.

In August, the players who would form the Soviet national team for the series against the Canadian professionals from the World Hockey Association were chosen. We began training specifically for this series of games but knew practically nothing about our prospective opponents.

The Soviet papers were filled with speculation about Billy Harris's team. Many experts even predicted this team would be better than the National Hockey League all-stars we played two years earlier. In my mind, I thought back to those earlier games against the Canadian professionals, going over the details again and again.

Senior hockey coach of the Central Army Sports Club, Konstantin Loktev.

I was aided by a reporter who called one afternoon and asked, "Would you like to hear excerpts from the books which appeared in Canada after your series against the NHL all-stars?"

"Of course," I replied.

Until then, I had been familiar with only one such book, *Hockey Showdown* by Team Canada coach Harry Sinden. Excerpts from this book had been published in *Komsomol Truth*. The reporter introduced me to *Faceoff of the Century* by Gilles Theroux and *Hockey Night in Moscow* by Jack Ludwig. Some quotations from these books obviously deserve attention. Here, for example, is what the journalist Jack Ludwig wrote:

> "So there we were, this nation of puck-watchers, doing a countdown that would end on September 2, 1972, when 'the greatest hockey team ever assembled' would put on a dazzle no Russian had ever witnessed before. Canadian macho would be restored."

And so on in the same spirit.

I don't wish to harshly judge such obvious self-confidence. The Canadians have always considered their (and only their) hockey players to be the greatest of the great. More than one generation has believed them to be absolutely invincible. They never took us seriously and never showed any interest in what kind of hockey was played on the other side of the ocean. In all Canada, it seems, there was not a single person who doubted the professionals would win that series in 1972.

I remember how, having flown into Montreal, we were shocked at what the Canadian newspapers were writing. They seemed involved in a contest to determine who could frighten our team the most. One newspaper claimed the Canadian superstars could break through the boards with their shots. Another reporter insisted that the Canadians would have little trouble with the Soviet goaltender Tretyak because he was too young to stand up to the NHL. In a third story, a reporter promised to eat his article if we managed to score even one goal against the professionals. Incidentally, he later fulfilled his promise. The poor devil sat on the steps of our hotel in Toronto, placed a dish of soup on his lap and asked us to throw his shredded story into the broth. We were uneasy and we refused. The guy just fell into this stupid situation. Finally, he put the paper in the soup himself and ate it with ill-concealed disgust.

Here is another excerpt, this one from Gilles Theroux's book:

"When Tretyak was beaten after only 30 seconds, the crowd erupted and everyone knew the game would be a rout. We wondered what the Soviets were doing on the same ice."

That was a reference to our first game in Montreal in 1972. The noise was overwhelming. It appeared to me that mass insanity had developed in the bleachers. Shouting, banging,

"The noise was overwhelming. It appeared to me that mass insanity had developed in the bleachers."

whistling, sirens screeching, flashers flashing and an organ playing some sort of funeral dirge. Until this day, I have wondered how we kept from being completely confused by this din. The first goal by Phil Esposito set it off; the celebration was even more ferocious when Paul Henderson drove in the second goal. After that, everything fell into place. We became accustomed to the clamor and won 7-3, throwing our opponents into a state of shock.

I remember that Jacques Plante visited our locker room before that game. The best Canadian goalie of all time came with an interpreter and surprised us by explaining in great detail how I, the goalie, should play against Mahovlich, Esposito, Cournoyer, Henderson . . .

"Be attentive when Mahovlich is in the game," explained Plante. "He shoots whenever he has the puck—from any distance and from any angle. Come out to meet him. Remember, Cournoyer is the fastest forward in the NHL and Dennis Hull can drive in a puck from the red line. Also remember that the most dangerous player on our team is Phil Esposito. He shoots without winding up and can find the smallest crack in your defense. Keep your eyes on him when he is taking the faceoff—the defense can't cope with him in that position."

To make his instructions even clearer, Plante showed me all these things on a diagram. Then, he said good-by and left. I don't know what motivated his visit. Perhaps he felt sorry for me, a youngster about to be led to the slaughter at the hands of players such as Esposito. I don't know, but I thank Plante. His advice was very helpful.

There was much talk about hockey styles—the Soviet style versus the Canadian style. Jack Ludwig quoted Foster Hewitt, a veteran Canadian radio broadcaster, who suggested there was nothing new in our approach to the game.

"They say there's nothing new in the world," said Hewitt, "so perhaps we should look back to the style of the old New

York Rangers. That's the style the Soviets play so effectively—precision passing and smart team play."

Unfortunately, I have never seen the old New York Rangers and I am unable to judge how much their style of hockey resembles ours. But I am in complete agreement that precision passing and team play are the trademarks of the Soviet national team. However, we arrived at it in our own manner, without copying anyone, not the Rangers nor anyone else. Our hockey is original, and it is precisely because of this that we are the strongest in the world.

Jack Ludwig recognized this when he pointed to the great influence of Anatoli Tarasov on the development of Soviet hockey. Wrote Ludwig: "But poetic was the only word I could think of to characterize some of the things Tarasov had written on hockey. His statement, say, about teamwork—'a good pass must come from the heart.' Or his explanation that Soviet hockey players are good team men because they are not 'egoists.' Or his credo that the only revenge for dirty play is to beat the team of the guy who perpetrated the 'injustice.'"

Tarasov's comments are right. After the fourth game we played overseas, the Canadian fans began hooting at their team for the first time. After that game in Vancouver, Phil Esposito was interviewed on television. On my word of honor, I felt sorry for him. He was dripping with perspiration; his eyes were sunken and he seemed to be lost. In an insulted tone, he talked to the microphones before him and said, "I've put out 200 percent, and you people still aren't happy. We never knew the Russians would be this strong. Who could have known? All our lives, we've been told these guys are pushovers, but actually any one of those guys could sign with any team in the NHL."

The Canadian professionals were quite surprised that we, as a rule, weren't intimidated by the rough play which has always been one of the strong points of Canadian hockey. Finally, it is time for me to disclose a secret—the players of

"We weren't intimidated by the professionals—we had spent the entire summer specifically preparing for rough play."
Vladimir Petrov narrowly avoids a spill.

the Central Army Sports Club had spent the entire summer specifically preparing for rough play. The coaches had invented new exercises to condition us for the increased contact. They taught us not to be afraid of collisions. We arranged "cock fights" and even took boxing lessons.

There were lessons for both sides in that 1972 series.

Jack Ludwig wrote: "What is important is that the Soviet Union, on the basis of its performance in this hockey series and in past international matches, should have convinced us that it had something to teach us. It has something to teach us about preparation, about conditioning, about training, about coaching, about self-criticism and the criticism of one's teammates."

Theroux added: "First lesson: show respect for your opponent. It was a violent shock after the first game in Montreal which ended USSR 7, Canada 3, and only two days after the Russians landed here. The Soviet team was considered a mysterious one; mysterious in the way it could trap you into believing that they were coming here to learn from us . . . .We know what followed.

"Second lesson: Top physical shape. The Soviet players were ready and eager to play those eight games; the Canadian hockey players were not. It takes more than three weeks to blossom into good shape . . . .

"Third lesson: Try to learn from past mistakes. Coach Harry Sinden, in a reflective mood, said: 'We have to change our outlook on hockey here. I don't mean to change every aspect of our game, but many innovations could be incorporated into our style of play.

"'For instance, the passing play the Soviets have kept going all the time. The puck is moving from one side to the other, just like the players are. This style of play is not mastered in a few days, it has to be put into service, day in, day out.'"

And we? What did we learn from that first series? First, I couldn't get over how hard the Canadian forwards shot. Their shots were so strong! The Canadians were virtuosos with the puck and shot from any position. They were particularly dangerous when they had a rush. Phil Esposito scored most of his goals in that series when he was rushing; he was unstoppable. I think the Canadians were better shooters than we were, and this is one thing we can learn. Another aspect of the Canadian game which I liked was their fighting spirit. They always fought to the end which is the sign of an excellent team.

But two years had passed since that first series and now we were preparing for another confrontation with the Canadians. It was obvious the Canadians remembered that first series and had not been sitting on their hands since it ended. We had heard they were preparing for this series in a much more serious manner. We were expecting difficult games.

People are beginning to think of me as a veteran even though I am only 22 years old. What nonsense! I am far from being a veteran. Of course, I have gained experience and self-confidence during the past five years but there is always something new to learn.

I was first selected for the Soviet national team in 1969. I remember that season as though it were yesterday. In August of that year, I went to Sweden with the Central Army Sports Club team. The team took part in a series of friendly games, and then Anatoli Tarasov took me to a small town called Vesteros where the Swedes were holding a training camp for goaltenders. In addition to myself, there were eight Swedish goaltenders in the camp. We trained from morning until night and I worked very hard. I wanted to prove that I wasn't just a kid but, truthfully, I had a difficult time keeping up with the Swedes. For example, Holmqvist could run twice as fast as I. But I paid attention to the Swedish exercises and took notes on everything that happened. The trip proved to be very useful.

On my return to Moscow, our team took part in a tournament sponsored by the newspaper *Soviet Sport*. In the first game, we played against the Tractor team and we won 3-2. The next game was against the national champions, Spartak. I was sure that our number-one goaltender, Kolya Tolstikov, would play in that game, but a few hours before the game started, Tarasov announced that I would start. My knees began to shake. My teammates noticed my anxiety and attempted to calm me down, but I sensed they were not completely at ease with the coach's decision either. A mere boy would be defending their goal in such a crucial game.

The game began with the Spartak forwards putting heavy pressure on our goal. But on that night, luck was on my side. It seemed as if all their shots were aimed directly at me. The spectators began to applaud my efforts, even when I stopped an easy shot. They were obviously sympathetic to the boy who was defending the Army's goal. We won by 5 goals and I was the happiest person in the world. That evening, a television commentator said that Tretyak was the most valuable player in the game between the Army and Spartak.

That game dictated my future. Later, there were many grueling lessons in practice and in games. I tried to prove that my success against Spartak wasn't an accident, that I was really a goaltender. This was not easy because many people were skeptical of my age. There had never been a 17-year-old goalie at this level.

Before the traditional *Tass* tournament in December, Tarasov went to the training council of the Soviet Hockey Federation and suggested that I be included on the all-star team which would compete against the best amateur teams in the world. He received no support. One coach insisted: "Tretyak is too young; how can we depend on such a boy?" When Tarasov is convinced he's right, he has amazing powers of persuasion and can win anyone over to his side. Therefore, in the fall of 1969, I was on the all-star team of the Soviet Union.

September 1974

They were about to announce the departure of our plane, and once again I was saying good-by to my beloved city of Moscow. We were flying to Montreal, and then to Quebec City, for the start of our series against the World Hockey Association all-stars.

A few words about the World Hockey Association. This league was created quite recently but its owners, with the lure of huge salaries, have managed to entice a couple of dozen big-name players to jump from the National Hockey League. My old adversaries, Paul Henderson and Frank Mahovlich, were playing in the WHA. So were Bobby Hull and Gordie Howe.

Our team was excited. You could tell by the loud laughter and high-pitched voices. The excitement was understandable. Formidable opponents awaited our arrival in Canada, and the games ahead were going to be difficult. But one thing was clear—this was going to be great hockey, an intense struggle at the highest level.

The first series against the NHL players convincingly showed that there are no invincible professional teams. There is no longer such a myth connected with Canadian pro hockey. There is simply hockey, a game that is appreciated and played well in North America and in Europe. I think it is a good thing for hockey that we have destroyed the myth of

Canadian invincibility. I assumed that September that our opponents in the forthcoming series welcomed an opportunity to restore their prestige. I knew these games would be tougher than the first series. We would have to work much harder.

The games with the professionals, regardless of the cost, are undoubtedly good for hockey and, therefore, are necessary. Hockey, like every other living thing, can develop only through struggle. This law is immutable. I am convinced that soon games with overseas players will become as common as national championships are today. The Canadians are interested in these games no less than we.

Judging by everything, a new era is dawning in big-league hockey. We, the hockey players of the seventies, are fortunate in this sense.

In Montreal we changed planes for Quebec. It turned out that between the flights we had a free hour. The airport was besieged by reporters. They fired questions at me from three sides:

"Were you specially preparing for the games with the professionals?"

"Of course. Just like the professionals have prepared for the games with us."

"How do you evaluate Bill Harris's team?"

"In no way. We don't have any idea what kind of a team it is and how strongly it plays."

"Are you going to play just as hard as you did at the world championships in Finland?"

"We will act within the framework of the rules."

"What do you think will be the result of these games?"

"It will be favorable to the Soviet national team."

Having said this, I attentively looked at the faces of the Canadian reporters. Two years ago, my words would have produced sarcastic smiles. Now the reporters remained calm, as if I had said something that was obvious. What I had said, in fact, was that we would lick the famous unbeatable pros.

Later on, in Quebec, we saw the latest Canadian newspapers. It appeared that almost all of them were forecasting disaster for the WHA.

"How can they possibly win against the Russians when even the NHL all-stars could not stand up to them?"

We are staying at the Hilton Hotel in Quebec City and are training at the Coliseum, the site of the first game in the series. We are given a police escort when we go to practice. It's an unusual experience. Our bus rushes through the city without stopping, surrounded by policemen riding powerful Harley-Davidson motorcycles. Sirens are wailing, blinkers are swirling and we have green lights at every intersection. No one can pass us. People wave from sidewalks and cars as we speed by.

There is a large crowd on hand for our first practice. The entire WHA team has come to look us over. Boris Pavlovitch points them out to us . . . there, that's the famous Bobby Hull. And over there, there is the ageless Gordie Howe. Some we are able to recognize without any help: Frank Mahovlich, Paul Henderson, Pat Stapleton—we met them on the ice two years ago. The Canadians are nonchalantly chewing gum and staring at the ice.

"Let's show them what we can do," says Boris Mikhailov, as we leave the locker room. "We'll show them."

It is a tremendous practice. It is if we are on display, and we do our best. I defend the goal as if it were a crucial game—just to let them know we are ready. Our spirits are high. I just hope we don't use up our fighting spirit before the real thing begins.

September 17, 1974. It's the night of the first game and the Coliseum is packed to the rafters. The game hasn't begun but the crowd is already unruly. An electric organ is playing,

"It is a tremendous practice. I defend the goal as if it were a crucial game."

horns are screeching sharply and people are loudly beating on drums and kitchen pots. Although we were stunned by this silly cacophony two years ago, this time around, we are calm. You can make all the racket you want.

Personally, I enjoy playing before a large crowd. When the passions in the stands are raised, I feel a sort of lightness, an influx of strength and inspiration.

The game begins as the series began two years ago. The Canadians launch a successful attack on our goal, and we trail 1-0 after the first period. During the intermission, we receive instructions; we must outskate our opponents. Tempo, we must dictate the tempo.

We rally and then trade goals. The game ends in a 3-3 tie.

I have had to work so hard that if anyone had asked me how the game was going, I would have been unable to remember. For me, the whole game was a continuous shelling. It was if there were 10 pucks on the ice instead of one. But I think the Canadian goalie, Gerry Cheevers, probably felt the same way. He played a brilliant game.

There are two episodes in the game which I remember vividly. Serge Bernier shot at my net from a very good position. I blocked the shot and he broke his stick over the boards in disgust. Thirty-four seconds before the final siren, one of the Canadians—I think it was Mahovlich—suddenly came at me on a breakaway. As usual, I came out of the crease to meet the rush and the player became confused and missed the shot.

Bobby Hull scored two goals. No wonder he has become a legend. He has quite a shot. I hardly saw the puck. The defenseman Jean-Claude Tremblay was also outstanding. The best player on our side was undoubtedly Kharlamov. His breakaways should be filmed and shown to children as instructional material. He has come up from the Golden Puck competition to the highest level of hockey.

Valeri Kharlamov's career has developed in much the same way as mine. In 1962, when he was 13, Kharlamov and a group of his friends came to the Central Army's sports palace for the first time. He was the only one of his group to be admitted to the Army's sports school.

At that time, selections were made by Boris Kulagin. He was the one who saw the makings of a gifted athlete in Kharlamov, but it was Tarasov who provided Kharlamov with his higher education in the game of hockey. Now, Kharlamov is the greatest forward in the Soviet Union.

I have watched him play many times and have been impressed by the ease with which he checks opponents. He can do everything; he can maneuver at top speed, shoot accurately and cleverly pass to set up a teammate for a goal.

"I love to play beautiful hockey," he often says. There is no truer statement—Kharlamov's style of hockey is genuine art, applauded by millions of people. His signature is unique and brilliant; it is impossible to confuse Valeri with anyone

"For me the game was a continuous shelling."
Here Valeri Vasilyev comes to Tretyak's aid.

else. When he is on the ice, goalies tremble and the fans stormily express their admiration.

For the sake of justice. I must say Valeri has wonderful partners on his line. They are Vladimir Petrov, the Komsomol organizer for the national team, and the team's captain, Boris Mikhailov. For several years, they have been the premier line in Soviet hockey. They are all distinguished by an unquenchable thirst for goals. They can't accept defeat, even if they are only relaxing with a game of billiards or soccer. They simply have to win; that's the kind of guys they are.

Their tactics usually consist of overwhelming their opponents by moving the puck as if it were on a mad merry-go-round. They drive their opponents into a state of dizziness and confusion and then take advantage of this disoriented foe to drive home a goal. They are close friends off the ice and have complete faith in each other. It is not difficult to understand why they are the best forward line in Soviet hockey.

The game is over. We sit in the locker room tired and empty. There is absolute silence.

"That's some bath we're taking," I think to myself. "Some veterans we are! It appears as if these games will be more difficult than the previous ones. We are not going to have a cakewalk across Canada. Hold on, Vladik!"

Our reserves, the players who did not dress for this game, join us in the dressing room. They were sitting in the stands during the game and they appear very excited.

"That's some game," says Volodia Polupanov, "that's . . ." He tries to continue but he is unable to find the words to express his thoughts. "It's just unreal," he finally blurts out. The rest of us just sit in silence until someone says, "Give us a chance to catch our breath, Volodia."

"I have never seen such hockey!" someone shouts from the corridor. Neither had I.

"We sit in the locker room, tired and empty."

"Well Vladik, how many times did you save the team?"
asks my double, Alexander Sidelnikov. But I just sit there
quietly, completely exhausted.

Later that evening, Bobby Hull appears on television.

"The Russians have a good team," he tells the interviewer.
"They are like an army platoon, disciplined and united.
Everyone is aware of his responsibilities. I think our team, on
the other hand, was a bit nervous. McKenzie told me before
the game that his knees trembled from nervousness. But now
we'll get hold of ourselves. Our boys will win this series."

"We shall see, we shall see," says Sidelnikov as he turns
off the set. As usual, we are sharing a room. We don't talk
much. That's not because we have nothing to talk about; it's
because I usually clam up before the games. I become remote
and silent. Sasha knows this and tries not to bother me with
idle chatter.

Every goalie has his own method of tuning up for a game.
For example, Konovalenko can play solitaire by the hour.
Sidelnikov does not seem to make any specific preparations
and remains calm, imperturbable. I turn inward. During the
day of the game, I think only of the game, nothing else. I
keep telling myself: "You must play well, you can't betray
your team."

I have to remind myself, "You are a goalie. You have a
special responsibility. You are the most important player on
the team."

During the day, I try to take a nap. I don't like to talk
because I don't want to disturb my concentration. As game
time approaches, I join my teammates for black coffee.
Everything that surrounds me ceases to exist unless it is
related to the forthcoming game.

On the way to the rink, I don't notice anyone. Some
people take offense when I fail to greet them. They say,
"Tretyak is like a blind man, he doesn't see his acquaintances
and doesn't recognize his friends."

Other players appear more human. Maltsev strides into the

arena with a morose look on his face, but as he hears voices call, "Hello, Sasha," from all sides, his stern face softens and he returns the greetings. Yakushev is preoccupied but polite and says, "Hello," over and over while Vasilyev smiles at the girls who wave to him.

But Tretyak strides straight ahead, hiding under a mask of silence, a soulless machine. It would be useless to address me at such a time. I would just walk by without answering. Perhaps, I would even lower my head further and walk faster. There is no point in being angry with me, I'm already on the ice, in the thick of battle. There is time to exchange greetings and talk after the game.

When I describe my preparations, I'm not talking about a superstition or a thoughtless habit. When I'm preparing for a game, I don't allow my mind to rest. On the contrary, I keep thinking about ways to play better. I was taught to prepare myself this way by Tarasov.

He would say, "A goalie must be able to win the game. Do you understand what this means? Learn to think rapidly, analyze your opponent in an instant. When he is still thinking about where to shoot, the goalie should already know where and how to stop the puck. Remember, you can't be a good goalie if you don't have intuition. But intuition doesn't come by itself; you have to think continuously."

> *Question:* What is the most important quality a goaltender should possess?
> *Tretyak:* The ability to stand up, no matter how difficult it is. The puck is not made of cotton or fluff, it can hurt. But a goalie must learn to endure that pain.
> *Q:* Which shots give you the most trouble?
> *T:* The most difficult shot for me is a screened shot from a distance because when an opponent is in my path, I can't see the puck in time to react to it.
> *Q:* When you miss a save, do you blame yourself or credit your opponent?
> *T:* I blame myself.

Q: What kind of relationship do you have with your fans?
T: I appreciate them and greatly respect those who appreciate hockey.
Q: Does a goaltender have to be a good skater?
T: Absolutely! He has to be a virtuoso on skates. A goalie doesn't always stay in one place, he is always in motion. The best skater among our goalies is Alexander Sidelnikov, who once played forward for the Soviet Wings.
Q: In your opinion, who has the better chance on a penalty shot—the goalie or the forward?
T: I think their chances are equal.

The second game of the series is being played in Toronto. The highlight for me comes with an opportunity to block a penalty shot. I will explain about that later.

Toronto is one of the centers of professional hockey in Canada. Almost everyone in the city is a hockey fan and the games generate a lot of enthusiasm. It is also a city which holds few good memories for me.

Two years ago, we played the second game against the NHL All-Stars and lost 7-3. Tonight, the score is 4-1 against us; no one can explain it.

After the first game in Quebec City the coaches scolded many of our players, particularly those on defense. I

"A goalie must learn to endure pain."

expected us to play better tonight. But what has happened is a shame.

I think one of the problems is the size of the rink. North American rinks, and Maple Leaf Gardens in particular, are not as wide as European rinks. Our team is used to wide-open action; we also like to pass and skate behind the net. In Toronto, there is no room to maneuver. The distance between the net and the boards is only one meter—hardly enough room for a forward to race through it. We are also having problems with the technical play of our defensemen. Vasilyev and Gousev, for some reason, are not backing each other up in the usual manner.

After the second period, I am very tired. The Canadians have put tremendous pressure on me and, for the first time, I go to coach Konstantin Loktev and tell him: "I don't know if I'll last."

"You must endure, Vladik," he replies. "You are our only hope."

I return to the ice for the third period, feeling as if I have had no rest at all. And what happens? I am challenged immediately in those first few seconds of the period when Johnny McKenzie breaks away and bears down on my net like a mad bull. I immediately tune in and forget about everything else. All I see is McKenzie, and I look at his eyes and the direction of his swing, hoping that he will give me a clue to where he will shoot the puck. Somehow, I make the save.

It goes on from there—shot after shot after shot. I must say most of the Canadian attacks seemed pointless. The Canadian players will wait until they are nearly in the crease before they shoot. They do not try to deceive me or entice me from the crease. No, they just come out and swing as hard as they can—as if they are attempting to put the puck right through me. This is what I describe as the straight-forwardness of Canadian hockey.

Where has my fatigue gone? I play as if I were

unconscious. Perhaps, it is inspiration, but everything in me feels sharp. I haven't allowed myself even a second of rest, which may be to the good because I think if I weakened for even a second, my sharpness and inspiration would disappear.

In the final minutes, the Canadians are awarded a penalty shot. It is an interesting situation. According to our rules, any player on the team may take the penalty shot. But in the professional rules, the shot must be taken by the victim of the infraction or by one of the players who was on the ice when the infraction occurred.

I don't know this, so I expect to see Hull or Howe take the shot. Instead, I look up and see a tall, lean player at center ice—a Canadian completely unknown to me. Later, I learned it was Mike Walton.

"Well, I think to myself, "if he is entrusted with the shot, it must mean he is their best shooter or a master of feinting and faking." Often, I wonder in such situations whether I can block the shot, but now I don't think of anything. Everything becomes dim. All I can see is the opponent and the puck, nothing else. Until the attacker crosses the line, I can do nothing. But as soon as Walton crosses the line, I jump out to meet him. My aim is to cut down the angle, to cover the largest possible part of the net. I move forward so rapidly that the Canadian becomes intimidated and hurries his shot. I welcome that kind of shot. The stands erupt in a howl although I'm still not sure whether it was from annoyance or in appreciation of my efforts.

When it is finally over, Walton comes to me and says, "Good game!"

"Thank you," I reply weakly.

As we return to the locker room, my legs give out. I drop on the bench completely exhausted. It's all over and all I feel is deathly exhaustion.

Many questions swarm in my head. Will I be able to stand up to many more of these prolonged attacks? Will the

"Waiting for a penalty shot, all I can see is the opponent and the puck, nothing else."

defense finally straighten itself out? Is it possible the Canadians will play all the games at this hurricane pace? How can I deal with Hull?

I am also puzzled about an apparent goal by our Volodya Petrov. The Canadian referee Brown disallowed the goal after he lost sight of the puck. Later, while flying to Winnipeg, I asked him about the decision and he apologized.

"Please don't remind me," Brown said, shaking his head. "Of the 20,000 people in the arena, I was probably the only one who didn't see the goal."

Our players took this obvious injustice with dignity. I wonder how the Canadians would have reacted if it had happened to them?

In the two games against us, the Canadians have used two pairs of defensemen. Without a doubt, the better pair is Pat Stapleton and J. C. Tremblay. They are cool and calculating. They rarely attack, but I think that Gerry Cheevers, the Canadian goalie, is very happy with their style.

It was interesting to read Tremblay's thoughts on this series in a Toronto newspaper.

He said, "I never trained as persistently as I did before the games against the Russians. I devoted the whole summer to getting in shape. I ran every day and lifted weights. When we arrived in training camp on September 1, I weighed 10 pounds less than I did at the same time last year. I have never been in such good shape."

I can believe him. Our opponents were obviously very strong and they were playing better than we were. They were playing with enthusiasm and dedication. Every one of them was ready to block the puck with his body, even the veteran Gordie Howe. It seems that the Canadians have also come up with a winning strategy. They have disciplined themselves to play defensively and then counter-attack—the same tactics we used so successfully two years earlier.

It is the pace that surprises me the most. I can't believe that our opponents will continue to play at such a high pitch.

Before the third game, we assemble without our coaches for the traditional Komsomol meeting. We know that if the Canadians win tomorrow's game, it will be very difficult—in fact, almost impossible—to win this series. We meet with one another, look into each other's eyes and say the stirring words which mean so much to us. We talk about our country, our millions of fans, about the great hockey tradition we represent. We are addressed by Komsomol organizer Petrov, by our captain Mikhailov and others. We are reminded of the task before us.

On the night of the game, the arena in Winnipeg is filled to capacity. The profiteering outside before the game can't be described. Ten-dollar tickets are being sold for $200. There is an air of excitement for the Canadian fans and even the tone of the press has changed drastically. It appears that the Canadians now believe the WHA all-stars will beat us.

Winnipeg is the city in which Bobby Hull plays. He's one

"We look into each other's eyes and say the stirring words which mean so much to us."

of the greatest Canadian players of all time and one of the most good-natured persons I've ever met. Hull is an example of endurance and patience. He works tirelessly. I was not surprised to learn that he is also a farmer and raises cows. Although he is 35 years old, his game has lost none of its freshness and daring. He can do everything in hockey.

I learned he has been using a hockey stick since he was 4 years old and he became a professional when he was 18. It is interesting to note that Hull, unlike his teammates, comes to all our practices and watches attentively. He and the other millionaire on the Canadian team, Gordie Howe, are an example for the other players. They stay in the same hotel rooms as the others and are the first players on the ice for practices and warm-ups. With their modest behavior, they seem to be constantly reminding the rookies how real hockey players should behave.

For the third game, we dress our best players. Kulagin tells the reserves, who were also chafing for action, to have patience.

"After we win a couple of times, and prove that we are stronger, then everyone will play," he says. I don't know about anyone else, but our coach is confident of victory tonight.

There is one significant change for Team Canada—Billy Harris has started Don McLeod in goal. The papers said Cheevers needed a rest. I am glad to hear the series hasn't been an easy one for him either.

The ice is bad, full of puddles and lumps. Our forwards strike hard from the opening faceoff. They are beating the Canadians to the puck. As I expected, the Canadians aren't able to keep up the pace they set for themselves in those first two games. They begin weakening while our boys, to the contrary, seemed to regain their past prowess.

I have another run-in with Walton in the second period. He unleashes a violent slapshot which catches me in the stomach. The shot is so hard I cringe with pain and become nauseous and dizzy. But I stay in the game. There's no time to think about the pain as Henderson breaks in on the goal. Hold on, Vladik!

Between the second and third periods, our team doctor, Oleg Markovitch Belakovski, gives me some pills to kill the pain. We are leading 7-2 at the time, and I am confident the coaches will put Sidelnikov in goal for the final 20 minutes. But no, I have to go out again and, for the first time, I have taken a drug to help ease the pain.

I suffer for 10 minutes without allowing a goal and then come to the bench where the doctor has prepared a cloth soaked in ammonia. I smell the cotton and sneak a look at the coaches. Surely, they will replace me now. But no, I have to play to the end. I feel lousy as I return to my net; I'm sure I will faint.

I allow three goals in the final 10 minutes. The first is

scored by Henderson; it's interesting because he had several better chances in this game. He came at me several times and took shots in what I regarded as a very primitive manner. He had opportunities to pass to a teammate or tease the goalie but instead he simply wound up and shot as hard as he could. I blocked all his shots without difficulty.

Finally, I see him skating furiously toward me. The game is already won, and I see our defense dozing off. I can depend only on myself. There is another Canadian to Henderson's right, in a much better position to score, and I'm sure Henderson will pass. I think to myself, "He has to do it. It will be stupid not to pass." I begin to shift to the side of the other Canadian, leaving the other side of the net slightly open. But Henderson has no intention of passing to anyone. He takes the shot and hits the open side.

Again, my biggest problems come from Bobby Hull. Occasionally, I don't even see the puck when he shoots. It comes like a bullet. But there is more to Hull's shot than that. Usually, when a player shoots or flips the puck, an experienced goaltender can determine the direction of a shot and its speed by the angle of the player's windup. This swing takes only a fraction of a second for a high-class player, but I can usually cover the area where the forward is aiming. But Hull shoots without winding up. His terrifying slapshot is performed almost casually, with a simple wrist motion. It's no surprise to learn he is one of the top goal-scorers in hockey.

Hull's teammates seem to play only for him. Many times, I find myself confronted by McKenzie and Andre Lacroix as they move toward our goal. They are both quick and daring but, frankly, I scarcely pay attention to them. I look for Hull. Where is he? As usual, he is slowly sneaking up to my net. McKenzie and Lacroix are passing the puck to each other but I guarantee that neither will even think of taking a shot. They have some magic faith in Hull and it is he—and only he—who will take the shot. He gets into position, the puck is passed to him, he shoots and again I have to make another big save.

In Moscow, Hull will be guarded very closely and he'll score only one goal. But in the games in Canada he scores six goals. From one game to another, I attempt to find a counter maneuver to use against Hull. I finally decide that I will have to come out to meet him sooner—not when he's coming into our zone, but as soon as he gets the puck. That's what I do in those last four games.

Canada's final goal in Winnipeg is scored by Walton. The shot is extremely hard. I catch the puck but in some inconceivable manner it slips from my glove and flutters into the net as if it is alive. And that's how it finishes, with our team leading 8-5—a beautiful, decisive and difficult victory.

Once again, the Canadian newspapers praise us by saying: "Anyone who doubts we are playing against a great team is plain stupid. We have not seen a single Russian who could not play in the NHL."

Of course, it is pleasant to hear such high praise for our game, pleasant to know that we are the strongest. Canadian hockey, which was until recently like a mystery hidden behind seven locks, has been unmasked by us. We can now understand its traditions, its excessively rough nature. We have found its weak points, and I like to think that on occasion, we have taken advantages of those weak points rather well.

The Canadians have also benefitted from these international series. Two years ago, Team Canada coach Harry Sinden said to everyone within earshot, "We must change our view of hockey. We don't have to scrap everything, of course, but there must be some innovations. First of all, we can borrow the Russian concept of team play."

The Canadians are very quick to learn their lessons. Most

of the WHA players have been instructed in moving the puck around, and their tactics are much more diversified than those of the team we played two years earlier. Billy Harris has taught his forwards to fake and to move the puck into a good position before shooting. Only Hull and Henderson have remained faithful to the old style.

I have always been interested in the reasons why Canadians prefer to play without helmets. Once I asked a professional about it and he admitted, "It's a stupid and reckless habit."

"There are so many injuries in our game," he continued, "and each year there are a number of players who resolve to wear helmets. But, once the season begins, we take them off. We wear helmets right up through junior hockey, but professionals have never worn them. I think that's part of the problem. It's become a distinguishing mark of a pro to play without a helmet, and it's a difficult tradition to break. Eventually, I think we will all realize the danger and wear them. For now, it's just a few players like Tremblay."

I like the Canadian goalie Gerry Cheevers. He is a skillful as well as an outstanding sportsman. Before each game, he comes up to me and taps my pads with his stick, wishing me good luck. The one thing I can't understand is that he smokes. Even before the game, one can see him in the locker room with a thick cigar between his teeth. I once asked him why he smoked and he replied that it helped him keep calm.

While I'm talking about players, I wonder why Johnny McKenzie plays so rough. He is always looking for someone to hook or to push, and he doesn't even try to hide the fact.

"Yes, I play rough," he says, "but I don't mind if someone plays rough with me." Personally, I don't like such a philosophy and I don't like McKenzie. He's a bully.

Anything can happen on the ice. But when the game is over and passions are calmed, we shake hands and peacefully go our way. I extended my hand to McKenzie after one game, but he demonstratively turned away and, as if by accident, he painfully hooked me with his stick.

The fourth game in Vancouver ended in a tie, 5-5. In my opinion, it was a fair score. It was a long, hard-fought game and there were only 4 minutes remaining when Maltsev fired the tying goal. It happened on a faceoff in the Canadian end. Cheevers and Trembly were talking to each other as if they had forgotten the play was in progress. Maltsev got the puck and fired it with lightning speed at the Canadian net. A Vancouver newspaper summed up the winning team by writing, "When the Russians have an opportunity, they don't waste any time."

Everyone remembers what happened next. I won't go into detail about the games in Moscow but will simply remind the reader that the series ended in a resounding victory for the Soviet national team.

First we won the fifth game which, as everyone knew, was crucial. As we put our game together and began believing in ourselves, the Canadians went downhill. They were exhausted. They had already squeezed the last ounces of strength from their bodies and only seldom showed their former skill and enthusiasm. It was obvious they hated to lose, but the Soviet team won three of the four games in Moscow and one was tied.

The stakes in this series were very high for the WHA team. They knew the credibility of their league hinged on their performances against us. The competition between the two leagues is fierce, and one could almost imagine the NHL maliciously rubbing its hands and celebrating a WHA defeat. The intensity of this rivalry may have been the cause of the rough play in the sixth game. The Canadians needed a victory at any cost.

Before the seventh game, our coaches heard a rumor that the Canadians wanted to "eliminate" Tretyak. "Take care of

"My heart ached, worrying for our players—particularly my replacement, Alexander Sidelnikov."

Vladik," coach Boris Kulagin told my teammates before the game. "If one of the Canadians even touches Vladik, don't let him get away with it." But the warning was unnecessary —everything went all right.

I didn't play in the last game. I sat in the third row of the stands with my wife and watched the game from a new perspective for the first time. It was strange, because my heart ached, worrying for our players—particularly my replacement, Alexander Sidelnikov. There was no reason to be concerned. Our team was superior to the professionals; the victory would have been even more decisive if Cheevers had not played so well.

So we proved to be better in this series of games against the Canadian professionals. Our Soviet national team won four games. Three games ended in a draw and we lost only once. We outscored the Canadians 37-27.

The games played in the arenas of Canada and Moscow weren't simply between two hockey teams; they were between two different styles of hockey. We won and I think that proves that our style of hockey is more up-to-date, contemporary. It proves that the route we have followed during all these years is the right one. The new coaches of the Soviet national team, Boris Kulagin and his assistants Konstantin Loktev and Vladimir Urzinov, are brilliantly continuing the victorious traditions of their famous predecessors, Anatoli Tarasov and Arkady Chernyshev, who retired in the spring of 1972.

In these games, we gave all we have—and more. We displayed the best qualities of Soviet sportsmen: team play, devotion, unity and will to win. In my opinion, we looked better than the Canadian professionals in all aspects of the game, particularly in speed. The Canadians were obviously unable to cope with the tempo which our team set from the very beginning and maintained throughout the series. The professionals were also undermined by their tactical

"Canadian goalies come out further than we do, but I think Soviet goaltenders are superior in close combat. We are better prepared to stop a close shot."

limitations. Soviet hockey has proved to be more creative and more artistic.

It is difficult to compare myself with the Canadian goaltenders. They play the game differently than we do. They come out further and often start rushes by passing ahead to their defensemen. This is something they are taught to do from childhood. But I think Soviet goaltenders are superior in close combat; they are better prepared to stop a close shot.

After this memorable series, we received a memorial pennant which had been in outer space, the gift of the National Leninist Communist Youth League (Komsomol).

Questioner: What did the games with the Canadians mean to you?

Tretyak: They toughened me. It was real hockey!

Q: Did you like the Canadian goalies?

T: They are good guys. They know their business down to the last detail.

Q: Is it true that the Toronto Maple Leafs had a goalie named Terry Sawchuk, who did not miss a single puck in 110 games? They also say that in 16 years he received 400 stitches in his face.

T: I do not know about the stitches; it is possible. In regard to the 110 shutout games, it sounds like a legend.

Q: What are your plans for the coming season?

T: They will, for the time being, be related to the Soviet national championship. We Army men want to be best in the land once again.

March 1975

Spring has come again to Moscow. The last snow has melted in the city. Many boys have put away their skates and have switched to soccer. But hockey continues for us.

In a few days, the world championships begin in Munich and Dusseldorf. The circle will be completed. It seems as if we were fighting for the world championship in Helsinki only yesterday, but a year has passed. A year—for me, it flew by like a day—a year that was both difficult and happy. They say it is easier to become world champion than it is to hold the title. If this is so, then we aren't going to have an easy time of it in Germany. Our top rivals, the Czechs, have never been stronger. Last week, we were matched against them in a tournament for the *Izvestia* prize in Prague and we lost three times. Our team has never suffered three defeats in a row. But the Czechs were brilliant. They raced around the rink at a mad pace and were still completely in tune with one another. Their goalie, Jiri Holecek, was calm and in control of the situation; he received excellent support from his defense.

Upon returning to Moscow, we were subjected to endless criticism. "The offense is not producing. The defense is asleep. Tretyak is unrecognizable." Some hotheads even recommended that we be severely punished for our performance.

We actually looked bad on the ice in Prague. Very bad. To be frank, almost every line played poorly. Could it have been different? No, it couldn't! Our entire team appeared to be off form, but it was a natural and inevitable phenomenon. We were very tired, and the fault lies with the overcrowded schedule in hockey today. Many players were so tired by the spring that they should have been sent to a rest home instead of to a championship series.

Personally, I could barely move and I felt uncomfortable, insecure in the crease. I experienced nervousness and, for the first time in a critical situation, I felt something akin to panic. My hands wouldn't obey my brain's command, my mouth was dry and my legs were like cotton. I was feeling the effects of the long season—the high-tension games against the pros from the WHA, the New Year tour, the *Izvestia* tournament and the difficult battle for the Soviet national championship. During the entire season, I stood in the nets without relief, showered by a hail of pucks and experiencing terrible nervous tension. It is possible that some of my teammates are even more exhausted. For example, I know that Petrov's line in particular is feeling the effects of the long season.

I am not complaining. Please understand me. I simply wish to explain why the Soviet national team stumbled so unexpectedly three times in a row in Prague.

Our coaches realized that we were tired, so before the *Izvestia* tournament they arranged for a rest in the form of a tour of the German Federal Republic. The coaches did the right thing, although perhaps we could have used even more relaxation. While on the tour, we were still required to travel and play, yet the competition was not very difficult. But, as they say, the coaches know best.

The coaches were faced with two choices. The first, which we selected, was to take a break and then gradually build strength as we moved closer to the world championships. The second method would have been to maintain peak form throughout the season, through the *Izvestia* tournament and through the world championships. Because we were deathly tired, this method would have been completely unreasonable. The coaches did the right thing by sacrificing the *Izvestia* prize and preparing us instead for the principal series of the year.

At this point, it might be a good idea to let you see what we went through between the tough series against the WHA all-stars and the world championships. As soon as the series against the Canadians was completed, we entered our regular league competition, leading to the championships of the Soviet Union.

Before the New Year, our Central Army Sports Club team travelled to Canada for a series of games against junior and senior amateur clubs. To tell the truth, we looked upon this series as a breather. After all, the Canadian amateurs aren't as good as the Canadian professionals, and we expected to take care of them quickly. Alas, it didn't turn out to be a breather. Our opponents practically climbed out of their skins to beat us. In every game, we were forced to battle for each goal. Later, we found out that the clubs and the players had much at stake in this series. For the clubs, there was great prestige in being able to say they had beaten a Soviet team. There was an even greater motivation for the players. They were 18- and 19-year-olds hoping to attract the attention of the professional scouts. Their zeal became understandable when we realized that good performances could result in rich contracts later in their careers.

Our first game was in Hamilton. The rink there is so small that it should have been a children's sandbox rather than a hockey arena. We managed to win by only one goal.

The following day, I met the coach of the Toronto Maple Leafs and he asked me how I felt.

"Pretty bad," I replied, waving my hand.

"I can feel for you," he said. "It's easier to play in a telephone booth than that sardine can in Hamilton."

In Toronto, we again experienced great difficulty before defeating the Marlboros, the local junior team. The Canadians played as if there were a million dollars at stake. There was a sellout crowd on hand, and the papers on the following day wrote that the Russian athletes had provided the Canadians with a lesson in hockey. They called our game beautiful, lyrical and contemporary.

When we were in Toronto, we visited the Hockey Hall of Fame. It is a most beautiful museum! Here, one can find out anything one could possibly want to know about hockey. The exhibits include many well-known Soviet players and coaches. One of the most prominent exhibits is a huge wax model recreation of the final seconds of the eighth game between our team and Team Canada in 1972. For Canadians, this was a moment of great happiness. With the score tied 5-5, Paul Henderson scored the goal which decided the series in their favor.

We played seven games in Canada, won all seven, and finally returned home exhausted. But there was no time to rest. We immediately resumed our quest for the Soviet national championship. It was during this next period that we suffered a series of spectacular defeats.

We had been having problems on our club with the second and third lines. Petrov, Mikhailov and Kharlamov had played exceptional hockey, but they weren't made of iron and they became tired. It was not surprising—they were on the ice for more than half of each game. When these players had an off-night, there was no one to pick up the slack.

There was still a wide gap between these masters and the younger players. A possible exception was Vladimir Vikulov who never failed to give his best effort, even in this difficult time. The 29-year-old Vikulov is a marvelous sportsman with a fine feel for hockey. For many years, he was our Komsomol organizer. He was a perfect choice for the job because it would be difficult to find a more serious and conscientious athlete.

Vikulov has been a member of two Olympic-gold-medal teams as well as several world championship teams. If he had linemates of the same stature, this line would be priceless. Unfortunately, he plays with two youngsters—Victor Zhlutkov and Boris Alexandrov—and they lack Vikulov's experience and maturity.

Zhlutkov and Alexandrov are examples of the nation-wide popularity of hockey. Zhlutkov is a native of the small northern town of Inta, while Alexandrov learned to play hocky in the distant Kazakhstan city of Ust-Kamenogorsk which is 4,500 kilometers from Moscow. The winters in this area are very severe and temperatures sink to minus 45 or 50 Celsius. But the boys of Ust-Kamenogorsk are not afraid of the cold. There is a hockey rink near every house, and there are two or three teams in every neighborhood. The final children's competition for the Golden Puck is held in a beautiful arena that accomodates 5,000 fans. The winners are decorated with medals, and the best team receives a trophy and a hockey stick autographed by the members of the national team.

Ust-Kamenogorsk is not unique in this respect. Hockey is just as popular in Zhlutkov's hometown of Inta, or in Gorki where the goaltender Victor Konovalenko lives and which produced Valeri Vasilyev—now the top defenseman on the Soviet team—or in distant Khabarovsk where Gennadi Tsygankov was raised.

But I was speaking about Alexandrov. This fellow has caused quite a bit of trouble for his teammates and his coaches. He is only 19, unsettled and difficult to handle. He has some beautiful qualities, such as talent and perseverance, and we are all anxious to see him develop into a good hockey player. He continuously improvises on the ice. Occasionally in practice, even I find I am no match for him. He notices the smallest crack in my defense and shoots with precision. As we say, he is always "loaded" for the goal. He could be a worthy replacement for Kharlamov in the future.

The problem is that Alexandrov's temper occasionally betrays his youth. He can be cocky and lose his self-control. He has behaved like a spoiled star. Perhaps, it is our fault. We have let him get away with too much. Once he was accepted on our team, we figured he was so young that it wouldn't hurt to spoil him a bit. As a result, he has gotten out of line. In several games, his rambunctiousness has landed him in the penalty box. The penalties have been deserved—but they have also hurt our team.

At the end of January, we asked Alexandrov to the Komsomol meeting. He heard quite a few unpleasant words from his comrades. Our team is honest and united; we don't tolerate conceited athletes. The meeting decided to suspend Alexandrov for two games. Boris asked for the floor and appeared quite upset as he promised to improve and begged us to believe him.

I have been watching Alexandrov closely since this incident, and I'm glad to see that he is straightening out. I hope that we won't have to worry again about Boris Alexandrov.

Why am I telling all this? I think that this episode with the young forward provides an insight into the spirit of our team. To me, this is quite revealing. We are always aware of the high demand on a player's moral and spiritual qualities, of a player's responsibility to his teammates. This is the secret of the unity of Soviet hockey players, the secret to their victories.

> *Question:* What kind of character should a goalie have?
> *Tretyak:* He always has to be tough, fired up by the game.
> *Q:* Is a goaltender's height important?
> *T:* I'm 6' 1", but there are many goalies who have been short. One of the greatest goaltenders in history, Victor Konovalenko, was short. The Canadian goalie Gump Worsley is short, as is Gennadi Lapshenkov. The short goaltenders are more nimble and have the advantage on low shots. On the other hand, they have to come out of the net further to cut down on the angle, and it is much harder for them to cover a high shot.

Q: Is there much danger involved in being a goaltender?
T: I don't think any position in hockey is any more dangerous than another. I believe the goalie receives more injuries in practice than he does in a game. During practice, shots are coming at him from all angles; he doesn't have time to react to every one. They used to say that a smart player won't play goal. But the prestige of a goalie is much higher now, and that has changed.
Q: How do the players react when you allow a goal?
T: Some scold me as if I had let the puck through on purpose. Others come up and tap me on the pads, as if to say, "Don't worry, Vladik. We'll score five goals to make up for this one." I don't understand players who criticize the goalie. The goalie has to be encouraged and helped. Taking him to task for a mistake can wait until after the game is over.
Q: Is it true that it is very important for a goalie to be able to relax at times on the ice and then also be able to mobilize his forces very quickly?
T: Yes, that's true. It's necessary to watch the puck at all times and react accordingly. For example, when the puck is at the other end of the rink, I can relax and conserve my energy. When it is in our end, in the corner, I'm plugged in about 60 percent, because I know the puck can't be shot from that position. When it's passed out front, I'm plugged in about 95 per cent. Finally, when someone shoots, I'm using 100 percent of my capabilities. In this sense, the ideal goalie was Konovalenko—he had great concentration.
Q: Is there a danger in leaving a rebound?
T: There certainly is! In many cases, it means giving up a sure goal, and the most accomplished masters at finishing off such plays are the Canadian professionals. In general, the ideal solution is to catch the puck. If this can't be done, you should either direct the puck to the side or cover it with your body.
Q: What can you tell us about discipline in hockey?
T: Discipline, the ability to keep oneself under control at all times, should be in the blood of every sportsman. It should be developed from earlier childhood. I will illustrate this point with an example from my own experiences. In 11 years with the Central Army Sports Club, I've never missed a practice. I've never even been late. I'm used to going to bed on time and have sacrificed other interests to concentrate on keeping all my affairs in order. I have taught myself not be rude and

"In general, the ideal solution is to catch the puck."

not to give in to rudeness. This discipline has to be applied equally to all. It's wrong to forgive some for tardiness and other infractions while others are severely punished.

Q: Do you get tired of hockey?

T: I do. But one month away from the ice, one month of rest, is enough to make me want to go back.

On the day before leaving for the world championships in West Germany, the Soviet national team followed tradition by visiting the Blue Room of the newspaper *Komsomolskaya*

Before leaving for the world championships, the Soviet national team followed tradition by visiting the offices of the newspaper Komsomolskaya Pravada.

Pravda . It's our oldest tradition; we observe the Russian custom of "sitting before going." At this time, we received the good wishes of our journalist friends and assured them (and their 10 million readers) that we would uphold the honor of Soviet hockey.

I am not a superstitious person, but I find it curious that we attach so much significance to this gathering. In 1972, we placed second at the world championships in Prague. There were many reasons for this, but somehow we all recalled that before going to Prague, we had not come to the Blue Room. We just hadn't found time for a visit in all the commotion. Or perhaps the new coaches were unaware of the tradition. As I said, it's not superstition, but the Soviet national team does have traditions which shouldn't be violated. In essence, most of them signify the strong bonds between Soviet hockey and its fans.

In the Blue Room of *Komsomolskaya Pravda*, we were given the usual flowers and souvenirs. We were also presented with a puck which had been in the paper's museum for the past 11 years. It is the puck with which the Soviet national team scored the winning goal against Canada in the 1964 world championships. In return, the journalists asked us to bring them the winning puck from the 1975 championships.

On the next day, we flew to Munich. Several weeks later, we returned, carrying the winning puck in our luggage.

December 1975—January 1976

Superseries. This is the only name to describe the coming series with two of our clubs (Central Army Sports Club and Soviet Wings) matched against the strongest teams in the National Hockey League: *Superseries.*

It's not an original name, but what's important is that it truly reflects the significance of these games. This will be the first time we meet the professionals at the club level. The circumstances have touched off a great deal of speculation. Everyone is trying to guess who will win the Superseries. Our fans besiege us, but what can we tell them? We simply tease them by saying the strongest team is going to win. Of course, we are confident of our strength and are crossing the ocean with far different feelings than we had in 1972. As far as predictions are concerned, however, we would rather leave them to the fans and the reporters. None of our players even tries to guess the outcome of a series—at least not out loud. That's our custom.

The old year is rapidly drawing to a close and, as usual, we're going to greet the new year far from our homes. Christmas and New Year's Day are family holidays all over the world, just as they are in our country. But these traditions we hockey players regularly violate. While everyone is sitting at the table surrounded by relatives toasting one another with champagne, we are somewhere on

Tretyak, home at last with his family.

the other side of the world, and we can hear the voices of our wives, children and parents only by telephone. But what can we do, such is the life in sports. The end of December is the peak of the hockey season and has traditionally been reserved for lengthy overseas tours.

Like everyone else, I like to look back over the previous 12 months. This year didn't turn out badly at all. I can consider my program a 100 percent success. The Soviet national team won all 10 matches to take the world championship in Munich and Dusseldorf, having defeated its top rival, the Czechs, 5-2 and 4-1. My club, the Central Army Sports Club, won the championship of the Soviet Union for the nineteenth time, clinching the title well before the season was over. The government decorated many hockey players, and I received the Honor Medal in a ceremony at the Kremlin. Sportscasters again selected me as the year's best hockey player. I won't hide the fact I take devilish pleasure in these honors.

In another six months, I will graduate from the Institute. My two-year old son, Dimka, has learned to use a hockey stick and insists that I play with him.

One day before practice, I'm stopped at the door of our locker room by a man with a hefty package. He introduces himself as a representative of the Moscow publishing agency Progress and hands me a package.

"Here are several copies of a book by Ken Dryden which we have published in Russian," he says. "We would like to have your opinion of it."

The book is called *Hockey at the Summit* and is an account of the 1972 series. I am filled with pleasure as I relive the excitement of three years ago. There's one paragraph which I have read over and over again:

> "The Russians obviously are interesting guys. It would be great to talk hockey with them. Talk about anything. But there is no way. I'd like to ask them what they think of Canadian professional hockey players. Are they impressed with us or not impressed? And in what ways? Sadly, there is no way for me to find out. Press conferences only produce diplomatic responses, the type interpreters have memorized. So I learn nothing. Here are guys for whom we have a new-found respect; now they are sitting only twenty yards away, and we can't even talk to them, although we communicate a bit by hand signals."

You're right, Ken. I know that everyone of us feels the same way. It's a pity that our interaction was confined to the rink. We could have told each other lots of interesting things. The purpose of sport is to bring people together, and I never thought that this was just mere words. But let's be completely honest, Ken. In 1972, we were separated by more than the language barrier. Many of your friends were unable to swallow their pride. To them, we were "pitiful amateurs" or "chicken feed." They looked down on us. It took time for you to respect us, as you say in your book.

What do we think of the Canadian professionals? My notes should answer Dryden's questions to some extent. We think that they are excellent athletes and, with a few exceptions, excellent guys. We also think that we can play hockey with them on an equal footing and that regular series between our two brands of hockey assures progress for both the amateurs and the professionals.

Prior to leaving for Canada, I at last felt that I had achieved fighting form. Until then, my game hadn't really come together. But finally everything fell into place and the puck behaved as if I were its trainer. The newspaper *Soviet Sport*, commenting on the national championship game between our club and the Soviet Wings, wrote, "Tretyak undermined all the opponents' plans. His solid play psychologically destroyed the Soviet Wings' forwards."

I felt great. Even the veterans on our club marveled: "Vladik, you look as if you were reborn." Actually, I won't go into many details about our battles against the NHL teams. They were televised and reports of who scored and how were published in newspapers. I doubt I was able to see more from my goal than you could on the television screen. I have, instead, elected to give you my impressions of different games and to share with you encounters outside the arena.

By the time we arrived in Canada, the Canadian and American newspapers were no longer writing that the hosts would "devour" the Soviets, but most North American observers favored the professionals. Therefore, I was surprised to pick up a copy of *Journal de Montreal*, one of the largest papers in that city. The headline read: Raise your hands to salute the Russians. Underneath, there was roughly this prediction by a hockey writer:

> "Do you want my prediction? I favor the Soviet players. I think they will win five games, lose two and tie one. Obviously, I would like to be proven wrong, but. . ."

"By the time we left for Canada, I had finally achieved fighting form. I felt great."

As far as I know, this journalist was the only person in Canada to correctly forecast the result of this series.

My first feeling in Montreal is that of terrible cold. There's a raging blizzard and the wind makes it seem even colder. The time differential also affects us a great deal. We are aching all over, and for some reason we're extremely thirsty. Could it be from the change in diet? We are staying in the Queen Elizabeth Hotel, and we're constantly sought by reporters.

"Why do you prefer a wire mask to a plastic or plexiglass model?" I am asked by one television reporter.

"It has obvious advantages," I reply. "It is easier to breathe with the wire mask, and it is also safer. All the goalies on our major teams are now wearing wire masks."

"Tell us, Mr. Tretyak, what do you remember most of that first game against Team Canada in 1972?"

"The first few minutes, when we fell behind 2-0; and the end, when the score was 7-3 in our favor."

"Has the style of Soviet hockey changed since the series of 1972 and 1974?"

"No. This style has produced many victories; why would we change it?"

"Would you predict the outcome of the coming Superseries?"

"Certainly. The result will be that, no matter who wins, these games will be beneficial both to us and to you."

The fanatical love the Canadians feel for hockey is well known. But things have changed. Before the 1972 series, their only heroes were their own stars. Now we can feel the difference. Policemen greet us with friendly smiles as we walk the streets of Montreal. The fans ask for our autographs and wait outside our locker rooms to greet us after practices. Even Harry Sinden, who was not disposed to be friendly after the 1972 series, has changed his tone. Here is what we read under his byline in a Montreal newspaper:

"The Russian strength is not only in their teamwork, carefully developed tactics and precise passes, but also in the fact they have capable players who play with daring and initiative. Someone compared Kharlamov with Rick Martin, but the Russians have quite a few other strong forwards besides Kharlamov—and how many Rick Martins are there?"

We should not take this praise too seriously. We also realize that we have more than enough deficiencies.

The Montreal newspapers are carrying interviews with the NHL players who competed in the 1972 series. The details of those games are relished, but nowhere is there a single word about last year's series against the WHA All-Stars. It is as if this professional league no longer exists in Canada. This seems to me proof that the feud between the NHL and the WHA is continuing, and Montreal is the capital of the NHL.

On December 26, there was a reception for the two Soviet teams at the Forum in Montreal. Afterwards, we went to our locker room to change and then to the ice for practice. All the Canadians tagged along to watch. It was not the same as it had been for the 1972 series. The Canadians watched attentively this time and took notes, their faces reflecting admiration and respect. I could not help but remember the arrogance and contempt we were shown by both players and officials when we first visited Canada in September, 1972. Where had they gone?

At first, we skated somewhat awkwardly in the Forum. We had to get accustomed to the small Canadian rinks. The building seemed very stuffy, too. What would happen during the game when the stands were filled with 20,000 fans?

"At first we skated somewhat awkwardly in the Forum. Canadian rinks are much smaller than rinks like this one in the Soviet Union."

On December 27, we flew to New York for a game against the Rangers. Early in the game we found ourselves having to catch up, but this only spurred on the Army Sports Club. We put on a fast and temperamental game. I think there were times when our opponents were confused and didn't know what was going on. Even their goalie was overwhelmed, unable to help his team.

"The way they move the puck had me dizzy," said Peter Stemkowski, after the game. "I looked around, and it was as if they were on a merry-go-round."

There were two unfortunate incidents in the Ranger game, but I refused to let either one bother me. First, a rotten egg was thrown from the stands and landed near my crease. I looked into the stands and saw the police collaring some character whose pockets were bulging. A policeman pounded on the pockets with his fist; I saw other fans holding their noses and turning away. It seems as if the pockets were filled with rotten eggs. Ah, I thought, he has a fine omelet.

As the game ended, someone threw a paper cup at me. I looked at him and then pointed to the scoreboard, saying, "Take a look at the score, you houligan." It was 7-3, our favor.

As we had expected, the best of the Rangers was Phil Esposito. He was also the best three years ago. In that first series, we nicknamed him "Phil the Bully." It seemed that in the 1972 series Esposito was unable to accept the fact that Soviet players were on an equal footing with the NHL. He was torn by frustration and, while his play was excellent, he often lost control of his passions. I can't say we parted friends.

In this 1975 game, Esposito showed more self-control, and it appeared he had recognized our right to play big-time hockey.

When the owners of the Boston Bruins sent Esposito to the New York Rangers, we were surprised. We asked about this transaction when we were in Boston and were shocked to hear that the Bruins considered this deal favorable to them. "It is important to get rid of an aging player," we were told, "because in a little while nobody will be interested in him." There you are!

Yes, our old friend had changed. He didn't skate as fast as before but his brilliant technique, his ability to change direction and stop on a dime, and his instinct for the goal were still his trademarks. After the game, he said, "I warned my teammates to watch out for the Russians, but they laughed at me."

As we left New York the following morning, we were again greeted by glowing accounts of our performance in the New York newspapers. Said one reporter, "Perhaps it is not we but the Russians who invented hockey. In any event, that is what it seemed like yesterday on the ice at Madison Square Garden. It was none other than Boris Alexandrov who showed the Rangers how to play hockey."

On our arrival in Montreal, we went directly to the Forum for another practice. We knew that the most difficult games were still ahead of us. On December 31, we were scheduled to play the Montreal Canadiens in the Forum. They are the most famous team in the NHL—an institution that sets the standards by which all NHL clubs are judged. The Canadiens have won 18 Stanley Cups and their roster of players includes many of the greatest names in hockey.

One of the veterans on our team recalled that the Soviet national team lost 9-3 to the Montreal junior team (with the great Jacques Plante in goal) back in 1970. How was it going to be this time? Each one of us wanted to finish the year right. A difficult test awaited us that evening.

I can say, without exaggeration, that all Canada was anxiously awaiting this game. Scalping of tickets for the showdown had reached unheard-of proportions. It was unanimously agreed the Canadiens would give us our toughest battle.

"We must show the world that the best players are in the NHL," explained Montreal defenseman Guy Lapointe.

The reputation of Canadian hockey would ride on this contest. Not only the stadium, but the entire city, the entire country, was filled with electricity that night. The desire to win and to witness that victory had overtaken Montreal.

When we take the ice at the Forum, we are greeted by noise like I've never heard before. The reaction of the New York crowd was dead silence compared with this din! During the game, I always try to talk with my teammates, give them advice and encouragement. Here, it is inconceivable. I can't even hear my own voice—and the uproar is bound to continue through the entire game.

The Canadiens manage to break through our defense early in the game. They lead 2-0 after the first period. Our forwards are unable to organize a counterattack. We have no success with passing or our team play. The Canadiens hold the edge in shots-on-goal, 10-4. In short, the first period is a total loss.

Fortunately, none of my friends become panicky. In the locker room, the coaches urge us to skate faster in an attempt to tire the Canadiens. We are also encouraged to pass more accurately.

"It's going to work out," says Konstantin Loktev*. This is encouraging. It's good that even in the most difficult situations our coaches don't berate their players during a game. Even when they are annoyed and upset, we don't hear sharp words from them.

We start the second period at a disadvantage. Zhluktov receives a two-minute penalty. I really have to work! It seems as if the Canadiens are trying to exceed the limits of their talent. One shot follows another; they are all powerful and accurate.

However, we withstand the pressure and, when the team is back at full strength, Mikhailov cuts the margin by scoring our first goal.

The Canadiens go ahead by two goals again before the second period ends. One goal is the result of a scrappy play. Solodukhin and Gusev are in the penalty box and out of the play altogether. Our three remaining skaters try valiantly to defend against a strong attack, but Yvan Cournoyer breaks through. I never see the puck. There's a mass of bodies in front of my net; and I am screened as Cournoyer shoots.

But there goes Kharlamov! With agility and speed, he outskates Lemaire and Savard, then calmly decks Dryden with an accurate wrist shot. We trail 3-2 with 20 minutes to play.

The Canadiens again go on the offensive in the third period. Pete Mahovlich, Guy Lafleur and Cournoyer are all playing excellent hockey, hockey that is passionate, daring

*Loktev is currently a senior hockey coach of the Central Army Sports Club.

and honest. It is this last virtue I particularly wish to
mention. The game in Montreal left us with a very good
impression. In my opinion, this was really super hockey,
fast, filled with combination plays, tough—but not
rough—with an interesting and dramatic script. We go to the
wire before Alexandrov scores to tie the game at 3-3. I'm
convinced after this game that the Montreal Canadiens are
the strongest team in the NHL.

When it is over, the crowd gives both teams a long
ovation. I have said that I enjoy playing when the stands are
filled with people who don't spare the palms of their hands.
It seems to me that the game is even more interesting when
the crowd is rooting against me. There is inspiration in
having contact with the audience. I feel this inspiration most

"I catch the puck, fall on it, come up from a pile of bodies and note
that I'm still in one piece."

when an audience of thousands watches me without blinking and thirsts to see the puck shot past me. But I deprive them by catching it, deflecting it, falling on it. I come up from a pile of bodies and note that I'm still in one piece. Then I open my glove. Here is the puck. Then everything begins again. It was like that in Montreal!

A Canadian reporter and acquaintance once asked me why my best games have been against the professionals.

"Precisely because they are professionals," I replied without trying to be smart. "The stronger the opponent, the more assured I am in my net."

If there is anything that bothered me in the Montreal game, it was the many lengthy pauses for television commercials. While the players and fans were entertained by an organ, there was a fantastic amount of advertising. I think these interruptions favored the Canadiens, because our best weapon is a fast tempo; we can play an entire game without such interruptions.

"The stronger the opponent, the more assured I am in my net."

The morning after the Montreal game, I read approximately the following in the newspaper:

"Scotty Bowman, the Montreal coach, said his team hasn't had as many scoring opportunities in any game this season as they did last night against the Soviets. He added that any other goaltender would have been pulling splinters of missed pucks out of his skin like pieces of shrapnel. Anyone else but Tretyak."

Bowman credited my play with "stealing our victory," but that's not quite accurate. It was not I who stole the victory from Montreal. I just did my job well. All the others—Alexandrov for example—played just as well.

In North America, they feel Boris was discovered in the Superseries. For us, he is hardly a discovery. Even two years ago, Boris scored more goals on me in practice than Kharlamov. He is left-handed, and its's difficult for goaltenders to adjust to his shot. In addition, as I have noted earlier, he has great natural talent and is very persistent. On the ice Alexandrov improvises continuously and rarely misses a chance to score. All he needs to do is mature a bit faster and develop more self-control. When he accomplishes this, he will be one of the greatest.

After the game, we greeted the New Year at the Soviet consulate. I think that everyone was satisfied with the outcome. A few minutes before midnight, highlights of the game were shown on television. When the color commentator returned to the screen, he dumped confetti over his head and exclaimed, "Hurray, it's a tie. Happy New Year!" And so ended an unforgettable evening.

Most of the Canadien players declared later that they had played the best game of their lives. The sportscasters and spectators were equally enthusiastic. They said they hadn't seen a game like that in many years, although some thought that the home team should have won because they took 38 shots-on-goal while we took only 13. This reasoning can't be considered valid, however, because of the basic differences in the Soviet and Canadian styles. The professionals are taught from childhood to shoot without thinking, to fire the puck at the first opportunity. Our players, on the other hand, shoot only when they are sure. They like to carry the puck for a while, to play hide-and-seek with the opponents' defense and goalie. It is difficult to say which style is better; the optimum is probably somewhere between.

Boston coach Don Cherry recognized this fact after we played the Bruins. He said, "From now on, the number of shots-on-goal will not be a criteria for evaluating our players. What difference does it make if we outshot the Soviets 13-6 in the third period? They scored twice and we didn't get any. Shots-on-goal didn't mean much in this game."

We flew into Boston on January 5, several days before the game against the Bruins. We wanted to get settled because the series would be decided in Boston, and the Bruins were one of the strongest teams in the NHL.

Initially, we practiced at the main rink, but we moved to a smaller surface out of town because the refrigeration broke down at the Boston Garden. The rink in Boston is very old. If I'm not mistaken, it was built in 1926 and it is a huge, dim building. But for us, it holds one advantage over the other NHL rinks we've played in—it's larger, giving us more room to maneuver.

The Bruins, inspired by Buffalo's victory over the Soviet Wings, desperately wanted to beat us. Harry Sinden, currently the general manager of the Bruins, followed us everywhere. He brought his entire team to one practice session, and they sat by the boards and watched us intently. This gave us a bit of a lift, made us brace ourselves because we now had the feeling this would indeed be a very special game.

I repeat, the game in Boston would decide the series; both teams were aware of this fact. But the game was still several days away, and it was important not to waste energy worrying about it.

After our practice sessions, we generally went downtown. The weather was very different from Montreal—warm with no snow on the ground. We gladly accepted our hosts' invitation to attend a concert of contemporary music and a professional basketball game.

When I was alone, I prepared for the forthcoming game, analyzing the actions of our opponents and their strengths and weaknesses. This would be the first time we played the Bruins, but it was possible to construct an imaginary model of the game since they play typically Canadian hockey. I expected them to start very quickly, to storm our net from the opening faceoff. I saw the professionals employ this strategy in 1972, and it was not without success. One must be prepared from the very start of the game. The first minutes can often be decisive.

Strange things do happen in the world. While we were preparing for the Boston game, we received several Montreal newspapers and were surprised at their contents. There, in black and white in the latest issue of the *Montreal Star,* was an article which said the Canadiens had dispelled the myth of Soviet invincibility. In *La Presse* we read the following: "The Soviet system is no longer a miracle. It's possible to find the key to it." Everything had turned topsy-turvy! Who would have thought that the professionals, who so recently had been considered the world's greatest players, would now describe our game as "a miracle" surrounded by a "myth of invincibility"? Who would have believed it three years ago?

We were anxious to learn whether or not Bobby Orr would be playing for the Bruins. He has been the brightest star in professional hockey and a great guy, something which we have had an opportunity to witness on several occasions.

We would begin training each morning at 10, and the Bruins would practice at 11, but Bobby was on the ice before either team. He had been off ice for three months because of an injured left knee and was receiving daily treatments following surgery, but they didn't seem to be helping much. Orr is a man who can't live without hockey, and that's why he trained like everyone else even though he was limping and cringing with pain.

If you can believe the newspapers, every game Bobby Orr has played in has been a great event in professional hockey. However, we have never seen him in action against our team. He has been beset by injuries, which I believe are still plaguing him.

We had time to become friends with this strong lad, on whose face there seemed to be a sincere and friendly smile. I only saw him with a sad expression on his face twice.

"They say I'm just afraid of the Russians and that I don't want to ruin my reputation by playing aginst them," he told us one morning. "It isn't true. I've dreamed of these games for a long time. Who could've known it would turn out like this?"

Bobby looked at his knee, and we tried to assure him that there were still many games ahead of us, many chances to renew the rivalry between our two systems.

"Come over to us and we'll fix your knee in a month," added our physician Igor Silin quite seriously.

As expected, the game begins with a furious attack on our goal. The Bruins are a strong team, even without Orr. They begin by checking and applying pressure all over the ice. The tempo is so great I wonder if the strength of our players will last very long, but we're familiar with the Canadian style now.

The Bruins have 19 shots in the first period. Valeri Kharlamov and Boris Mikhailov reply with a series of sharp attacks, but there are no goals.

The second period begins with a gross mistake on my part. Forbes takes a long shot, and the puck ricochets off my stick-hand glove. All it takes is the slightest lapse in concentration and the puck flutters into the net. It's been a long time since I've committed such an error.

But it seems as if our opponents have exhausted themselves. Less than two minutes after Forbes's goal, Kharlamov ties the score. He scores again to make it 2-1, and Maltsev adds another goal before the period is over. Kharlamov, Maltsev, Tsygankov and Alexandrov appear to be all over the ice. Alexandrov scores the final goal in our 5-2 victory, neatly faking Boston goaltender Gilles Gilbert out of his net and connecting with a neat wrist shot. Even the pro-Boston crowd is humming with excitement at this play.

Remember what Don Cherry said about shots-on-goal? It's right there in black and white; they have 40 shots and we have only 19, but obviously we have taken the better shots in this game.

At this point, I would like to say a few words about the performance of our captain Boris Mikhailov, who missed part of the second period when he was struck in the chest by Wayne Cashman's stick. Mikhailov bravely returned in the third period to lead us. He didn't have a great scoring series, but he continued to be our team leader. It's difficult to imagine the Central Army Sports Club team without him.

After we beat Boston, a Canadian correspondent asked me about the game against the Philadelphia Flyers.

"We're in great form," I told him. "You saw the game tonight. If the Flyers don't get rough, the game will be as good as the one tonight."

Unfortunately, the last game of the series spoiled our good mood.

We attended a reception a few hours before the Philadelphia game, and our hosts already indicated they had no intention of treating us gently. The NHL champions were displaying a very unfriendly attitude. No one said hello; no one wished to talk with us. Even the Philadelphia newsmen seemed put off by this obvious animosity.

On the left, Boris Mikhailov, captain of the Soviet national team.

Everybody saw what happened next. There was no hockey on this night in Philadelphia. The Flyers accomplished what they wanted but their 4-1 victory was tainted. It isn't something they earned.

Many hockey authorities have expressed similar opinions about this game. The great Bobby Hull, for example, said he was indignant over the Flyers' play. "They give us hockey sticks so that we can bring enjoyment to the fans," said Hull, "not so that we can slaughter our opponents."

The New York Times called this game a "triumph of terror over style." No one can accuse this paper of being sympathetic to the Russians.

Only the coach of the Flyers, Fred Shero, tried to defend the thesis that his team deserved their victory. Shero, who once came to Moscow to study our hockey systems, displayed a reasoning completely devoid of objectivity. I am quoting his comments as published in the *The New York Times* several months after our game:

> "The Philadelphia Flyers are not a band of cutthroats. We are the best hockey team in the world. We were criticized . . . because we are the best team. It's just that we have more guts than any other team."

Perhaps, this is Fred Shero's usual style, but I find it rather amusing. Let's read further:

> "We did not brutalize the Russians, nor have we ever brutalized any team. It is true that we do get more penalties than other teams, but that is not because we are animals or goons. It is because we have more courage than any other team . . .
> "And because we have the courage to hold our ground, trouble sometimes starts. Yes, even fights. We do not go looking for fights. But, if challenged, we fight. That's part of the game, too."

Permit me a question, Mr. Shero. What do you mean by courage? Do you mean blows from behind, kicking, tripping? Is that it? You have written that the "Russians were overwhelmed" and this, presumably, is the result of a Philadelphia team "playing with discipline and patience." It's true that we were overwhelmed but for an entirely different reason. We have been schooled in a system which understands the morality of hockey and which rewards the values of endurance, courtesy and fair play. We simply did not know that a band of cutthroats on skates could, before thousands of spectators, have an open season on hockey players and not be punished.

It was a revolting sight. When our coaches took us off the ice in the first period because they didn't think we could continue to play under those conditions, we were sure that we were not coming back to the ice that night. Not a single player on our team wanted to continue. Any one of us could have been seriously injured by a foul blow. What kind of sport is that? It has nothing to do with true sportsmanship.

Our team returned to the ice only after lengthy assurances by Philadelphia officials that the game would continue according to the rules. But by that time, we had lost interest in playing hockey; there was no enthusiasm left. We were just trying to see it to the end and hoped there would be no other horrible incidents. Yes, the Flyers achieved their objective, but can their victory be considered just?

I don't think the Flyers are the best in the NHL, even if they have won two Stanley Cups in a row. On January 11, 1976, the Flyers demonstrated their usual style and proved they were the absolute champions of the world—in penalties and brutality. Even by professional standards, their style is monstrously rough. If they always win in this manner, and it appears to be so, how can they be the strongest?

Despite the Flyers, we won the Superseries. The Wings also played well and our combined record was five wins, two losses and one tie. Once again, Soviet hockey showed the world its winning formula.

September 1976

After a vacation in Crimea, I was called before the
Committee for Physical Culture and Sports, which manages
all sporting events in our country. At the committee
headquarters, an old-fashioned mansion on the sidestreets in
Ekaterinij near Arbate, I was told to get ready. "It is likely
that you will soon be going overseas again to participate in
the Canada Cup," they said.

"All right," I answered. "I will be ready." Frankly, I had
mixed feelings about the news. On the one hand I was eager
to compete with the professionals, those masters of hockey.
It would be tempting to submerge myself in the thrills of the
incomparable competition, knowing I was not exactly the
worst on the ice. I looked forward to checking myself—my
skills and my character—would everything be the same as
before? Yet, on the other hand, there were disturbing factors.
The most serious problem would be the make-up of our
team, which was even then practicing for the games in
Canada.

During the summer our best player, Valeri Kharlamov
(I think he is the best forward in the world) had met
misfortune. While driving home, his car had crashed when
he lost control on a sharp curve. The car was in smithereens;
Valeri and his wife were rushed to a hospital. The report was
not good. Kharlamov suffered broken ankles, ribs and a

concussion. The guy had just gotten married. Then, like that, his honeymoon trip was to the army hospital.

For some time, we wondered if Kharlamov would be able to play hockey again. He spent two months in that hospital bed. Valeri deserves credit: he held up magnificently. We didn't forget our friend. Somebody from the team was always at his side and letters came from all over the Soviet Union. These get-well wishes were better than any medicine the doctors prescribed.

In August, Kharlamov took the first steps on his own in his hospital room, but it was a far cry from being able to go out on the ice. Our national team for the Canada Cup was left without a leader.

The national team has usually been made up of men from the army and team Spartak players, coached by Shadrin. This season had been disastrous for the Spartaks; by September it was evident that Shadrin's team was in no shape to face the professionals.

All the injuries of 1976 probably influenced the Hockey Federation's decision not to send our first all-star team to Canada. Instead, the Federation called for an experimental lineup. Several little known rookies were to go with the team to Canada. The coaches chosen were Victor Tikhonov (who played for the Dynamo team in Riga), Boris Mayer (not long ago, he was the best skater of the Spartak team) and Robert Chernov (from the Chrystal team of Saratov).

As a rule, I have nothing against trying out rookies during a difficult game. It seemed to me, however, that our coaches had little confidence in these young players and that the rookies sensed this and interpreted their remarks as a putdown. The team was admonished as we left for Canada: "Your job is to be among the top three." Some of us felt that we were being told instead: "We know you aren't the strongest Soviet team and, therefore, we aren't asking you to do the impossible."

I don't think these parting words helped infuse us with

fighting spirit. As for me, I felt ready to meet the toughest rival. The other veterans on our team felt the same way. If only the rookies wouldn't let us down!

Once we arrived in Canada, I observed our novices closely.

Montreal! Mayhem, noise, an avalanche of predictions from the press! It was a heated atmosphere in both senses of the word. A sticky heat wave enveloped us, and it was hard to believe that it was already fall in Canada. The newspapers vied with each other in predicting the outcome of the tournament. Obviously, all of Canada felt the great importance of our meeting with the professionals. For the first time, the most powerful amateur all-star teams would face the professional all-stars. Everyone anticipated a breathtaking series.

Were our rookies confused by the noise and the reporters? No. At first glance, they appeared calm. They had strong nerves. We would wait to see how they did on the ice.

"If only the series was over!" complained Helmut Balderis. "Nothing is worse than waiting. Everyone is out of his mind with all the questions and predictions."

"True," I agreed. "The best answer we can give them now is by playing."

Twenty-four-year-old Balderis had been included on our all-star team after shining on the Dynamo team from Riga. He had gained fame for his speed and shots on goal. In fact, he might now be one of the best forwards in the game. "If this man from Riga and his teammates can skate together and find a common language on the ice, the best of the opposing goalies will have a hard time," I thought.

Balderis has been skating since he was four. He began his career as a figure skater, and they say he was pretty good. His first coach must be sighing bitterly now, thinking of the star figure skater he lost in Balderis. Helmut looks less like a hockey player than any of us. He is a typical student, bespectacled and slightly absent-minded, with fine features, quiet.

Outward appearances can be deceptive. Think of Bobby
Clarke of Philadephia. Looking at him, you might think he is
an inveterate cutthroat, yet once you know him you realize
that Bobby is the kindest, most good-natured sort of person.
We have become friends for good reason. Whenever we get
together, he asks about my wife and children. If we don't see
each other for awhile, he never fails to convey his regards
through our mutual acquaintances.

Before the Canada Cup tournament actually started, I was
invited to participate in a special exhibition arranged by
Canadian TV. I was told that the exhibition was given in a
small town near Toronto every year but that in the past only
the professionals had participated. This year for the first time
they would film an interesting showdown, I thought.

There were 16 forwards, 16 defensemen and 8 goalies in
the exhibition. For the Canadians, the goalkeepers were
Rogie Vachon, Dan Bouchard, Glenn Resch and Fred
Stephenson. The foreign goalies were Holecek (from
Czechoslovakia), Leppanen (Finland), Astrom (Sweden) and
Tretyak (USSR). Among the well-known professionals were
Bobby Clarke, Pierre Larouche, Rod Gilbert, Guy
Lafleur—who has recently been one of the highest scorers
in hockey—and many powerful amateurs were skating too.
Alexander Maltsev and Victor Shalimov were among the
Soviets in the exhibition.

It was very interesting to participate in such an event.
Much was new and exciting, and I was eager to compete.

The exhibition rink was cosy and somehow reminded me
of the Sports Palace of the CSCA. No spectators were
allowed in the stands. Everything was conducted under a
veil of strictest secrecy. There were TV cameras everywhere,
recording every move on video tape (the tapes were to be
aired on TV during the Stanley Cup finals). We were asked
to give our word of honor that we would not talk about the
exhibition or reveal its scores until spring.

To tell the truth, we began to get impatient with all of this, but thanks to the spirit of the other players, we soon enough felt at home on the Canadian ice. Although we spoke different languages, we became sympathetic friends quickly. An outsider might have seen us skating and thought we were members of one team rather than international rivals. That was wonderful!

First, a drawing of lots took place. The names of all players were placed in cylinders. The offense was to pick names from the cylinder containing the goalies' names, and we goalies were to pick from the drum containing the names of the offensive players. I drew Larouche. I knew immediately what this meant: Larouche, the 20-year-old rising star from Pittsburgh. Such a lucky Frenchman, whose happy future was apparently preordained! I don't know how Larouche felt, but I decided right away that meeting him one-on-one would not be easy.

After I drew Larouche, Denis Potvin aproached the cylinder to try his luck. He looked worried, and the Canadians teased him, shouting "Pull out Tretyak!" The poor fellow decisively pulled out a name, unfolded the paper and angrily threw it on the floor. Tretyak—everyone must have guessed it at once. I thought to myself, "At least I'll have one easier rival. Potvin has laid down his arms before combat has even begun."

Next we drew lots for the schedule on the ice. I prayed that at least I would not have to be the first to skate. The previous night I had hardly slept, trying to figure out how I would defend the goal in the one-on-one matches. I am seldom that nervous before a major competition, but I even worried about not representing Soviet hockey properly. Wouldn't you know—I pulled out "8:30." I would be the first to defend the net. No luck!

The defensemen competed first in the exhibition, being graded on their abilities to pass, on their formations and on their speed. Forwards were asked to perform a series of difficult exercises to prove impeccable command of their sticks and the marksmanship of expert snipers in shots on goal. Very few players were given high all-around marks. The judges even considered the quality of shots on goal, using special electronic equipment in the cage and crease.

At last the goalies were to be tested. Potvin faced my goal first. As usual, my nervousness disappeared as soon as I took my place on the ice. A whistle blew and Potvin rushed toward me with all his strength. I jumped forward about four meters to meet the Canadian. Disconcerted, Potvin shot prematurely. The puck landed square in my glove. All three attempts ended the same way: I missed none of Potvin's shots.

Larouche was tougher. He passed me on two out of three shots. His first slap shot was incredibly powerful and from far out on the ice. As Larouche took the shot, his stick broke! While I was looking for the puck among the debris, it slipped into my goal.

The final count was 4-2 in my favor. I didn't know how this would stand up since none of the other goalies had yet been on ice. Should I have been encouraged or sad?

I changed out of my uniform and went into the stands to watch the rest of the exhibition from behind the safety of the glass panels. With a cup of coffee I settled myself to await the final outcome.

Holecek looked pale and nervous. He probably hadn't slept much the night before either. He let five shots in total pass him. It was clear that I wouldn't come in last anyway!

When it was the Swedish goalie Astrom's turn, he let three shots by, saving three more. He probably faced a tougher job than the rest of us, defending against both Clarke and Gilbert—two very strong shots.

Since the Finn Leppanen also saved only three shots, he competed with Astrom in a playoff. The Swede made it to the semifinals. I also was in the semis, and we again drew lots to see which forwards we each would meet head-on.

I drew Darryl Glen Sittler. "That's something!" I thought.

Sittler had just driven in three goals in three tries against Holecek. (The Toronto Maple Leafs' forward later lived up to his reputation for speed and strength, making a good showing in the Canada Cup.)

My name was also drawn by Danny Grant, captain of the Detroit team and a man who had won his last two face-offs with the goalies in this exhibition.

They say that the devil is not as terrifying as we paint him. This was true of Sittler as well; his reputation exceeded his abilities. I managed to stop all of his shots, and I let by only one goal from Grant. That meant that my final score for the semis was 5-1.

I decided to go to the locker room and try to conserve my nervous energy for the finals. It was not easy waiting to hear how Astrom had made out against Larouche and Clarke.

Then the door opened. I could see immediately that Astrom was happy. Could it be that he had stopped six shots? As he approached, I demanded, "How many?"

"Three," he demonstrated with his fingers. "Three out of six." All the players had rushed in to congratulate me. "You won!" exclaimed Astrom. I had reached the finals.

The Czechoslovakian forward Hlinka was also in the finals. Among the Canadians, the goalie Stephenson and the forward Grant were still in competition.

In January, 1976, Stephenson had been the best goalie in our series. Now, however, Hlinka was able to score against him twice and Grant once. For some unknown reason, this calmed me down.

As I skated onto the ice, I talked to myself. "Now, Valdik, nothing can interfere with setting a record—six out of six. Forward!"

Hard as it is to believe, I stopped all six shots in the finals. I won the first prize among the goalies, and Hlinka was named best of the offense.

I later described these unusual competitions in Moscow, telling our coaches, managers and journalists how to set up such an exhibition in our country. It would undoubtedly be good for our goalies as well as for the offense, to say nothing of how the spectators would respond. They would be delighted!

I am sorry to say that our hosts for the Canada Cup must have wanted to win very badly, and it certainly looked as if they had stacked the draw in their own favor. We were supposed to play Czechoslovakia in the first round! In spite of our respect for the NHL, it was hard to accept this scheduling as mere chance.

A journalist in the *Toronto Star* editorialized approximately this way after the tournament:

> "We have to admit that the tournament was planned so that the Canadians had ideal conditions: skating on home ice with a high percentage of North American referees and a draw which favored Canada."

He went on to say that the Soviet hockey players had been called robots, even the executors of a giant Communist conspiracy to defeat innocent, clear-eyed Canadian heroes. But this Canadian writer thought that even if a conspiracy had existed, it would have been one organized by the Canadians. As far as I was concerned, if there were innocent skaters on the Canadian ice, they could only have been from the USSR.

We had to begin the tournament without time to adjust to the conditions or plot our strategy. Alas, my initial misgivings about the rookies were well founded. They were nervous and did not play well. Above all, they seemed to lack real fighting spirit, which has always been the strength of our national teams.

My job was difficult. The Czechoslovakians came at me several times one-on-one. Our defense scattered and couldn't put plays together. We lost this first game 3-5.

I have always admired the Czechoslovakian team. In April, 1976, we yielded the world title to them, having won the Olympics, however. The Czechs play with strength on all their lines and with good teamwork among the veterans and rookies. They have achieved a true fusion of experience and youth, presence of mind and fervent enthusiasm. Consider their goalies, Jiri Holecek and Vlado Dzurilla, who are well past 30 (incidentally, I was nicknamed Dzurilla at the beginning of my hockey career). It is premature to write these veterans off, however. Dzurilla, it should be mentioned, tried to retire in 1972 after the world championships in Paris. He was festively ushered out of the game, but four years later it became evident that the Czechs again needed this calm, conscientious and dependable man. They didn't have to beg Dzurilla. He gladly picked up his stick to begin what some say have been his best years on the ice.

The captain of the world-champion Czechoslovakians is Franticek Pospisil, one of the best defensemen worldwide. For their national team alone, he has played in nearly three hundred games. Boguslav Ebermann, the right wing, is swift and technically excellent too.

We weren't in a very good mood after our loss to the Czechs in the opening game. The papers were correct in describing us as 19 players but not a team. I was interviewed for TV and also admitted that what our team lacked was coordinated plays.

We then had to face the formidable Swedes. Although we were aware of their strengths and weaknesses, we knew that many well-known professionals would be playing on the Swedish team in this tournament. It would surely change their pattern of plays.

We tied the Swedes 3-3, letting victory slip away during the last minutes on the ice—in a most disappointing and unpardonable way. Kapustin passed the puck right to Borje Salming, who plays for the Toronto Maple Leafs. Our defenseman Kulikov was daydreaming, so Salming was able to pass to yet another Swedish professional Hedberg, who came at me head-on and deprived us of the victory.

The game was actually won during the first period when the Canadian referee made questionable calls against us. Twice we were left with only our three defensive players on the ice! There is no way to play three against five, and I couldn't help feeling that the referee had it in for us. My disappointment was only slightly mollified by being named the most valuable player of that game. The prize was given to me by Jacques Plante, who called me the greatest goalie in the world. Of course, such high praise from the mouth of the legendary Plante was very special, but I would have preferred to hear the whole team praised, not just one player.

After beating the Finns 11-3, we moved on to Philadelphia to play against the United States team.

I woke up in the Sheraton to a bright sunny morning. "It is going to be hot today," I told my roommate Sasha Golikov. "Very hot," he agreed. The day before the thermometer had shown 25° centigrade in the shade.

As we warmed up in the Spectrum, we were stifling, sweating like on a beach. Our hands slipped on our sticks, but we all worked hard. Victor Shalimov even put on his skates, although he hadn't completely recovered from a severe injury.

We beat the Americans with comparative ease (5-0), and I imagined that the rookies were gaining both self-confidence and skill.

The Canadians lost to the Czechs in the third period of their game, letting a puck get through and putting the Czechs into the finals for sure. Ahead of us was perhaps our toughest match, with the hosts.

Again our all-star rookies were tense on the ice. They played stubbornly, but at times they seemed almost frozen from nervousness. The first goal came in the eighth minute on a shot by Canadian Gil Perreault. Then Vikulov scored with an assist. Just before the break, Hull again led the Canadians in a strong play, and they scored. During the second period Barber brought the score to 3-1, and so it remained. I had to block more than 40 shots, but I have faced worse. I was in good shape. It was just a pity that our defensemen, who had started setting a fast pace, tired rapidly, making it easier for our rivals to score.

For the first time in many years, the award ceremony after a major international tournament would be held without the Soviet all-stars.

The finals had matched the Czechs against the Canadians. They were the best on this hockey holiday and Scotty Bowman's team deserved to win the Canada Cup. I wouldn't say it was an easy victory though. The world-champion Czechs put up fierce resistance, and I thought they had a good chance to win. Nevertheless, at some moment their awe of the unbeatable Canadians got in their way. At the time, I didn't know, of course, that our third-place finish, so unusual for the players in red jerseys, would be repeated during the world championships in Vienna in 1977.

March 1977

Sportswriters often ask athletes how they feel about their fans. I answer such a question without giving it much thought since I have felt the same way about fans for a long time. I respect the real aficionados of course. It is hard to imagine Soviet hockey without these expert supporters. I should point out, though, that some fans are fanatics who, without considering the refinements of the sport, without understanding the game's beauty, spend days bragging about "their own" team, counting and recounting scores and shots on goal—and picking the players to pieces. How mediocre their discussions are! It is a good thing we don't have too many fans like this. They are just noticed a lot because of their loudness and rudeness.

In general, it is hard to describe the typical fan. There are people who wouldn't miss a single match, who stand in line overnight at the box office to get a few cherished seats to the important games. There are also fans who live where hockey isn't played, and they have only seen the game on TV but still know so much about the teams and plays that you might think they were born on skates. During the important tournaments, a type of chain reaction develops—only a few people can be found who aren't following the competition. A typical morning begins with the question, "What did you think of the game yesterday?" Even people who wouldn't

"I respect the real aficionados. It is hard to imagine Soviet hockey without these expert supporters."

recognize Kharlamov's face are heard to exclaim, "What a shot!" or "That was some match!" You hear hockey in government offices, in factories and shops and on the subway, from the mouths of the miners too. The fans are burning to give their impressions of the games and to rate the players. The sports sections of the newspapers are flooded with letters to the editors, who must clutch their heads wondering how to answer all of them (it is customary to answer nearly every letter to the editor).

You should read some of those letters! They contain whole treatises on "How to Train and Staff a World-Championship Team." In my opinion, children make the best fans; for one thing, they play hockey. More importantly, they don't look at hockey as just competition. They know that playing hockey provides a chance to master skills and beyond that to demonstrate nobility, courage and strength. I always answer letters from boys, since I know the joy it gives them to receive a reply.

Not long ago, some children made special gifts for me. A Moscow radio station had asked its youthful listeners to invent a new mask for Tretyak. Hundreds of designs came in. One second-grader sent a note with his mask: "I have been a fan of the Sports Club of the Army team since I was three years old."

Another boy gave me a mask looking like a pretty young woman's face (What a good idea! Who would shoot a puck into a lovely girl's eyes?). Most of the masks were scary, designed to be wolves or tigers or devils. One child suggested that I have a headlight installed in front of my mask to blind my opponents. Others offered to put earphones into my helmet so that I could communicate directly with the coaches. Finding out about all these projects and reading the letters has given me many pleasant moments. A few of the notes touched me deeply.

One boy wrote: "I don't know Tretyak personally, but Vladislav seems to be as close to me as a brother."

Another letter said: "When he is standing in the crease, life seems much more wonderful."

I am not really vain, but it is an undeniable pleasure to read such letters. I am indebted to my young fans.

In March, after our Army team had again become national champions—for the twentieth time—my teammates and I participated in a traditional series of meetings with hockey fans. We talked in auditoriums and factory clubs and to military units. Usually the halls would be overflowing with people who seemed very interested in inspecting us closely to see if our hockey skill and our purely human characteristics matched as they anticipated. We were asked every imaginable question.

> *Questioner:* How long does it take to change into your uniform?
> *Tretyak:* If I am not in a hurry, 10 to 12 minutes.
> *Q:* Will you say something about your fellow goalies?
> *T:* I've never met a goalie who was a bad person. An undependable, malicious or easily upset man, regardless of his talent, will never be able to protect the goal. It is hard to know the goalies—not only because their faces are covered with masks. Unfortunately, most of the fame falls on the forwards not on the ones who stop their shots. Could you, for instance, tell me much about Victor Singer other than that he has played for Spartak for 15 years?
> *Q:* Does your intuition improve over the years?
> *T:* Of course, experience helps develop good intuition. I have been rarely misled by my intuitions. As a rule, I know when an opponent has the puck just what he will do with it. There is no time for doubting and guessing. Hockey is a swift game.
> *Q:* Which sport do you find the most difficult?
> *T:* Racing on skis, both downhill and slalom.
> *Q:* Which athletes do you admire?
> *T:* I can't name anyone special. I am sure, however, that all national champions, world champions and Olympic champions deserve respect. It is difficult to become the best in today's world.
> *Q:* How would you feel about an athlete who never came in first but who spent himself, all his strength, and still finished last?
> *T:* No one could blame him. I would call that man a true sportsman.
> *Q:* Are your phenomenal reactions of any use to you outside of hockey?

T: My fast reactions have helped in driving on icy roads.

Q: Do your dream about hockey?

T: Never.

Q: How do you feel about the referees?

T: I understand that they have a hard time and that they are just ordinary people who can't be insured against making mistakes, but hockey is so passionate that I am unable to forgive a ref's bad call in the heat of the encounter. If you killed me, I couldn't pardon you—an unwarranted penalty against us makes me feel the same way.

Q: Can your composure, your concentration, be destroyed when you are defending the goal?

T: Probably, but I can't imagine how you would do that.

During such interviews, the audience is not composed of fans only. There are also hockey players, from factory or student teams, for example. Then technical questions are unavoidable.

Questioner: How can a goalie improve his reaction time?

Tretyak: I recommend ping-pong and tennis. These sports develop swiftness and good reflexes. They improve your coordination and they use the same muscles which a goalie needs in hockey.

Q: Is it good to try to pass the puck as you fall on it?

T: There is nothing good about that. You have to keep on your feet with confidence. A goalie who falls often, stopping the puck with his knees on the ice, is going to let other pucks pass over his head. Repeated sprints from the cage aren't good either. Frequent falls are a sign of absent-mindedness or just lack of skill.

Q: What does the goalie do when two offensive men are attacking and the goal is only defended by one man from the defense and the goalie himself?

T: The goalie's responsibility is for the skater who has the puck. His teammate can cover the second opponent and simultaneously interfere with the shot if circumstances permit. It is important for the defensive player not to rush from side to side trying to cover the whole rink.

Q: Do you watch the rival goalie during a game?

T: Yes. Of course, I notice his mistakes and his great saves.

Q: Which was the hardest game for the national championship this year?
T: I can say without hesitation that the four games with the Moscow Dynamo team were the most challenging.

Our national championships were held from October, 1976, through March of this year, and I cannot go into much detail about the games in this book. Our Army team did well throughout the series, especially in the early games. We lost only one game to Leningrad and tied one with Spartak.

Our team is well-tuned, but a friendly spirit governs our play. A soulless machine we are not. Consider Vladimir Petrov's fantastic persistence. In my opinion, he is the best center forward in the world. Look at the smart, fine game played by our captain Boris Mikhailov, irreplaceable in a striking line. Think of Valeri Kharlamov's and Alexander Gusev's devotion to the club, both of whom were badly injured and hurried back onto the ice, into the very hell that can be hockey.

After the New Year, our team fatigued for some reason. We were set back by the Tractor and Dynamo teams. Balderis shot four pucks into my net, and in the papers they said that Tretyak was afraid of the young star from Riga. That is not true, because I am not afraid of anybody. If I were, I would hang my skates on a nail. Balderis admittedly is a good forward, but for those four goals I have to put some blame on the weakness of my defensive line.

The turning point of the championship came during our game against the Moscow Dynamos. Playing for them were Alexander Maltsev and Valeri Vasiliev, and their coach is Vladimir Jursinov, a great hockey player from the past. The Dynamos were the only ones able to give our CSCA team an equal fight for the gold. Luckily, the third match between us was decisive.

We had been tuning ourselves to a fine pitch for this game. The Dynamo style is well known. They line up on the blue line, scramble for the puck and immediately attack the opponents with swift shots—it is too bad if their rivals haven't had time to retreat into their own zone—a sure goal. Our trump is also well known: attack! Loktev tells us to break through at high speeds, using long precise passes. For the Dynamo game, Loktev also chided me to watch Maltsev particularly. There was no need to remind me of this. I had already run a film of Sasha Maltsev through my head, reviewing how he shoots, from which points, how the whole game would surely flow through him.

Maltsev's teammates are also strong: Golikov and Prirodin. Watch out for them!

When the Dynamos skated onto the ice, they rushed about with great fervor, but we were hardly fooled. I noticed at once that they seemed worried and were just masking their nervousness with a show of bravery and bravado.

In the second period, our CSCA team was ahead, but the Dynamos tried hard to even the score. The tempo became maddening. I pressed myself into the ice as pucks seemed to fly at me from all directions. I didn't have a single minute to catch a breath. Maltsev had changed his tactics too—sly! Instead of circling around the cage looking for an opening, he had decided to go for the slap shot from farther out. The puck seemed to come out of a cannon. When the captain of the Dynamos has the puck, I am always involved, 100 percent.

Between periods I felt hardly alive. In our Sports Palace, you must cross a spacious hall with a cafeteria on the way to the locker room. Reporters, coaches and special honored guests kill time there until the action returns to the ice. You might see the chess champion Anatoly Karpov and not far away with a cup of coffee the cosmonaut Vitaly Sevantianov.

I could see reporters surrounding Antoli Firsov, who was assuring them the CSCA victory by three goals! I heard Tarasov and Chernischev discussing the game.

As I passed Anatoly Vladimirovich, I heard him tease a Dynamo player: "Why do you want this victory so much?

The Dynamos are not good enough to be called national champions." But Arcady Ivanovitch bragged back: "Wait till next year. Dynamo will show you how to play hockey."

Ten minutes of rest is not enough time for me to relax and yet tune up again for the hard fight in the net. With the team I move back toward the ice, walking on a rubberized runner. I don't distinguish faces or hear any more conversation. I am conserving everything for hockey—my strength, my stamina and my skill.

We followed our coaches' instructions precisely and pulled out the victory 5-2. Our men skated with fire, but we also skated with assurance and were completely reliable. That is the source of our club's success. Our twentieth championship was due not only to the fine skating of our veterans but also to some young players' efforts: Fetissov, Kabanov, Nurimanov. I like to watch how Yuri Moisev works with the rookies. He gives his soul and is as demanding as Tarasov.

The Dynamos won the silver and the Tractor team took bronze for third, placing for the first time. This made me feel good. It is interesting to play against this team from the Urals, which is swift, brave and single-minded—and continuously attacks. They had many shots on goal. I like that. They had previously been an awkward, straightforward team, but by 1977 the team had matured and had recruited some valuable new players. Still, their most appealing characteristic is their independence and aggressiveness.

Incidentally, I succeeded in blocking a penalty shot in the game against Tractor. As everyone knows, penalty shots aren't granted often. I had about ten chances to block penalty shots during the national championships and was able to block all ten successfully. The last chance was against Belousov, who skated toward my goal as I rolled out to meet him, knowing that this maneuver shocks a rookie. He lost his head, went to the right, shot. I lunged and blocked the shot with my stick. As I straightened up, I felt shivers running through my skin from the excitement and joy. Such moments are the best in a goalie's life.

Once the national championships were over, I had some time to spend with my family. My daughter Irenea had been born in December. I love to fondle her of course. Then, too, I had a lot of work to catch up on since I had decided to continue studying by going into research on the psychology of sports.

I was not permitted much vacation before returning again to train for the world championships which were to take place in Vienna.

May 1977

May has always been one of my favorite months. It is a
beautiful time of the year, spring filled with the smell of
lilacs. It is the end of the hockey season, the time of
championships and awards and an approaching rest. This
year, for the first time, May held some unwelcome surprises.

Probably all of my teammates felt a need to be left alone in
spite of the springlike days of May. We all felt a weight on
our hearts and needed time to think. It is impossible,
however, to hide from everybody. No matter where we
went, we heard the unmerciful questions: How could you
have lost? What happened? As if it were possible to answer
in two words why the Soviet all-stars came back from Vienna
with bronze medals!

We were not ready with an explanation for our poor
showing in the world championships. We needed time for
the excitement to pass, time to look with cool and calculating
minds at what had happened to us in Vienna. In the
meantime, we were all at the mercy of our emotions,
imprisoned by our passions and sorrows.

Our third place in Vienna was viewed as a tragedy by the
fans. Who could really blame them? We had accustomed
them to victory and taught them to believe that Soviet
hockey is the finest in the world.

Canadians started playing a primitive form of hockey in

the middle of the last century, and the first rules for the game were not formulated until 1879. The first European hockey championships were held in 1910. Ten years later in Antwerp hockey became an official Olympic sport. In that year, too, the first world championships were held. For the professionals, the Stanley Cup was first awarded in 1894; at that time, the game was only known in Russia by rumors.

It wasn't until the end of the forties that the Soviet Union put together a number of hockey teams, staffed mainly by soccer players and men who had played field hockey. In 1954, the first Soviet all-star team participated in the world championships, and that team won the title. Since then, we have captured the world crown fourteen times. Fourteen—something to be proud of! Our best years were from 1963 to 1971, when we took the gold medal nine years in a row. During that period, the national team was coached by Anatoli Tarasov and A. I. Chernov; we didn't lose until 1972. After our splendid win in Sapporo, Japan, during the Olympiad, we yielded the world championship in Prague to our hosts. Again in 1976, although we triumphed in the Olympics in Innsbruck, we lost to the Czechs in the Polish town of Katowice. In 1977, we had only taken third place in Vienna—how could it have happened? Why?

Memory takes me back to the beautiful capitol Vienna and to our sad performance in the competitions there. It would be far from the truth if I said we came to Vienna in a sour mood or unprepared. We were as well prepared as usual for international competition. Admittedly, I was psychologically tired and suffered from headaches from time to time in Vienna. I did not feel like thinking about hockey after having played a very difficult season almost without relief on both the club team and with the all-stars. Even against one's will, the head becomes muddled in such circumstances. I am not against one man defending the goal all season, but evidently in 1977 people forgot that Tretyak has never been made of iron and must once in a while have a break.

An interesting fight had been promised in Vienna. For the first time, besides the national amateur teams, the world championships would be host to teams from Canada and the United States on which professionals would be playing. True, the best professionals were not all in Vienna; many had stayed behind to play in the Stanley Cup series.

Ten years earlier, the Soviet team had taken the world title in Vienna. Only one member of that championship team was still on the ice to defend Soviet honor in 1977: Alexander Yakushev. He had been a rookie ten years earlier; in 1977, he was one of the strongest members of the team.

The series did not start badly for us. Among the teams we beat were the Canadians. Winning our first match against them was great. Unfortunately, the Canadians were not playing well as a team. In fact, I did not think they were taking the competition in Austria very seriously. One evening as we approached our hotel, we saw Phil Esposito clowning with a bottle in his hand and his hockey helmet slung low over his eyes. "Look!" Phil shouted. "Esposito in a helmet!" He banged his fist against the helmet. "How about that?" I only shrugged in reply. The International Federation of Hockey had ruled that all players in the world championships would be required to wear helmets on the ice for safety. Why make fun of it?* The rules should be respected.

The Canadians celebrated a lot in their rooms with wine flowing in rivers. We thought they were trying to show everybody how confident they were of winning, how they were the most famous, richest hockey players in the world. Somehow, they reminded me of schoolyard bullies.

*The tradition of not wearing helmets on the ice has been strong among North American professional hockey players, just as it was once strong among baseball greats. Courage and bravado have been associated with playing without a helmet's protection, but the prejudice against helmets is softening.

The Canadian team was rebuffed early in the series, losing to the Swedish team 2-4. I think they took the loss particularly hard. During the break before the third period I watched Larouche. He looked pale, disoriented—maybe embarrassed. He was chain smoking and drinking black coffee.

"Come on, pull yourself together," I told Larouche.

"Yes, we will show them," he answered, gulping his coffee as he ran onto the ice.

My friend was not able to show the Swedes anything; the Swedish team won handily.

An unpleasant incident occurred when the Swedish anthem was played. A Canadian player, Rosaire Paiement, demonstratively left the ice. It was poor sportsmanship and in bad taste, but credit should be given to the Canadian coach, Alan Eagleson, who ran after Paiement and nearly beat him up. I witnessed this scene involuntarily but noted several days later when we beat the Canadians that some of their team scarcely behaved better during the playing of our anthem. They leaned casually on their sticks instead of standing at attention during the national song, and I thought they were trying to show their disdain for us and were unsportsmanlike.

Our match against the Czechoslovakian team took place on April 28. It was then that I began to feel quite unlike myself on the ice. The rest of my teammates also seemed upset. We remembered too well the defeats we had suffered from the Czechs at the world championships in Katowice and at the Canada Cup tournament. Our coaches tried to calm us down, and I had to keep telling myself that I was in fact calm and ready to skate. Probably, the Czechs were just as nervous, for they surrounded their goalie and pounded on his pads, wishing him luck.

During the first seconds of play, Ebermann made a powerful shot to our cage, but I deflected it. Then I faced Bubla head-on. He shot; I put out my stick but had to fall on the puck, stopping it under my chest. It was a tense moment. Everything depended on which team could score first.

Luckily, during the sixth minute of play, Kapustin passed the puck along the boards behind Holecek's cage. Zhluktov took the puck and rushed the net, leaving Holecek helpless. We led 1-0.

It wasn't long before Martinec took a long shot at my goal. I was screened and didn't react quickly enough. The score was evened at 1-1.

We started the second period feeling stronger and sure of winning—and so it happened. Kapustin scored twice, Mikhailov and Babinov then brought the score to 5-1. In the third period, Yakushev put in the final goal, 6-1.

After the game, Novak, a Czechoslovakian player, said to me, "It is only right. You are the strongest team and will be the champions."

"We will see," I responded evasively.

On the way to the showers, Ebermann, clearly sad from the defeat, told me, "Well, we almost took the Canada Cup, but you are going to take this world title. You will see."

"You are probably joking," I interrupted. "The whole tournament is still ahead!" I really meant what I said, but the same couldn't be said of the rest of my team and of my coaches. They seemed sure the gold medal was ours already—but they were overconfident too early. Boastful interviews with the reporters, premature promises of victory to the fans who followed us to Vienna—this self-confidence was not like out team. It did us. in finally.

On May 2, we skated against the Swedish all-stars. All we needed was to win the match to nearly guarantee the gold medal. No one doubted our victory then. Big deal! We had beaten the Swedes many times in the past, and our team was already feeling like champions in Vienna. Certainly, our mistaken optimism was somewhat influenced by praise from the newspapers. The reporters were predicting that the title would be ours without question; they were saying that the championships were already over. Some of our players even began collecting sticks to autograph. If only our coaches had reminded us of the truth! If only they had put a stop to the celebrations until the time was really right.

The coaches' leniency could be understood. In six games, we had scored 64 times against our opponents. It was hard not to believe that we were an extraordinary team under the circumstances. One more victory was all that was needed after all.

During the first minute of play against the Swedes, Kharlamov narrowly missed the net. Soon enough, however, we scored. Strange as it may seem, this was not really an advantage. Because of that early goal, we thought we were really on our game and could relax and tear the Swedes to pieces.

Time passed without another goal from us. The Swedes scored once during the first period, bringing the game to 1-1. Our team was like fish out of water, flopping helplessly on the slippery ice. Try as we might, we could not recover— and the Swedish team was improving. The Swedes were shooting accurately and scoring without any interference from our defense. It was as if we played in a trance. Even short a man, the Swedes outskated us, keeping us away from their cage and counterattacking fiercely. The result was an astounding score of 5-1 against us.

At once the atmosphere in our locker room changed. In the place of complacency was nervous confusion. We were pumped by our coaches: "You must win the championship. You are obliged to take the medal for the Soviet Union. You must settle down and play better. You must bring the defense under control. You must . . . You must . . . You must . . ." A stranger hearing all this might have felt that we would face doomsday if we did not win the world championship title. Things did not look good. We had to face the Czechoslovakians next.

Dzurilla was chosen to guard the Czech goal this time. By the end of the first period, they were leading us 3-0. Sad and confused, we dragged ourselves to the locker room, not wanting to look each other in the eyes. No one would have recognized us as the Soviet national team. Vladimir Petrovich caught up with me and sniped, "You don't have to pass the puck to the forwards. You had better help the defense." I snapped back at him—it just wasn't like us to go after each other between periods. Our team was sick.

The second period brought the fourth Czechoslovakian goal. They were getting past our defense easily and shooting, always shooting. I was close to panic. "Get hold of yourselves, you guys," I was begging mentally. "We have beaten the Czechs tens of times—we are stronger!"

At last Kharlamov, Mikhailov and Balderis put in three shots, but we could do no more. Dzurilla was in top shape.

So, we had lost again . . .

Back in Moscow, I asked a psychologist if he had an explanation for our misfortune. He told me that I had forgotten what if feels like to lose. "When you give up a goal, or rather several goals, you begin to feel panicky," he told me. "You and your teammates forget the plays and each one begins doing only what he thinks must be done. Each person spends all his strength, but then there is no team on the ice. You forget to work together."

We were at an advantage against the Swedes, and yet we lost. I think that in addition to our problems on the ice, our coaches weren't able to give us real leadership when things got tough. Instead of rallying the team as a unit, they began to look for individuals to blame.

Losing to the Swedes and the Czechs didn't end the world championship series for us. We had to play Canada, who had tied the Czechs 3-3 and smashed the Swedes 7-0. Their fans had been giving them hell. Evidently, the Canadians had decided to take the tournament seriously and were playing in a way that justified their professional pride. Their early losses had made them band together; in the end, they really deserved better than the fourth place that they got.

Canada's supporters were really let down by the dirty play of the national team. I have seen a lot of things happen on the ice, but the "frolicking" Canadians skated in a way that would have benched us in the Soviet Union for a long time. Paiement, McKenzie and Russell behaved like houligans, so the referees had no choice but to slap penalties on them continually. While they were in the penalty box and their team left shorthanded, the opponents were able to score.

Our match with Canada on May 6 was no exception. It reminded me of the game we had played against Philadelphia a year and a half earlier. The Canadians must have decided to intimidate us the way they had psychologically attacked the Swedes. Even before the game, Phil Esposito was reported by an Austrian newspaper to have said he would grab an opponent by the throat, if necessary, to win.

During the warmups, a Canadian puck came into our zone, and Genia Tzigankov—a really good-natured defenseman—lightly passed it back, only to have the Canadian professionals descend on him like hawks. They wanted a fight. They wanted us to know how terrifying and bloodthirsty they could be.

Our warmup finally ended when a Canadian shot a puck directly at me. Frankly, I was shaken up. During my career, nothing like that had happened—no one had dared take a full hard shot at an unsuspecting goalie.

We had to take verbal abuse from the Canadians in the locker room, too—it was called psychological warfare, I guess. It was a loathsome scene.

After the game against the Canadians, I asked a friend who has worked for years as the Moscow representative of Air Canada what kind of a team they had brought to Vienna. Even he admitted being embarrassed by their roughness.

I remember well that during the game our Tzigankov had

made the first goal and soon the Canadians were shooting rapidly at my net. They shouted to upset me. I had to keep telling myself, "That is the last goal they will get." I didn't, in fact, let more than one puck get by me, which made the Canadians furious. Their provocation couldn't shake our defense after all, and the referees were firm in calling penalties. Even though Phil Esposito got hoarse arguing with the refs, the Canadians kept being sent to the penalty box.

We were making goals regularly in this game. Paiement was assigned to guard Yakushev and did so in an original way: by hooking Sasha's neck with his stick. Russell fought with his stick and then in the penalty box threw his helmet to the ground, breaking into a string of curses.

When the sirens at last announced that we had beaten the professionals 8-1, McKenzie punched Tsedrin in a fit of powerless anger, hitting him in the stomach with his hockey stick. What was the point? Did they hope we would scare easily and be afraid to meet them in future games or that the fans would applaud their pranks? The referees were fair and firm; we weren't shaken; the fans, on the other hand, began to chant, "Canada, go home!"

The Canadians claimed that the referees had called penalties against them unfairly, that the team had been keyed up and was edgy and easily provoked. It is true that the referees committed one serious error during the Canada-USSR game by incorrectly crediting us with the third goal in the Canadian nets. Even assuming that the referees were too subjective in this match, could their mistake have justified the Canadian aggression on the ice?

Admittedly, the world championships did not rest on our match with the Canadians. The title was really decided by our second meeting with the Swedes. A win would have given us the title; a loss put us into third place for the bronze instead.

After the cold shower given us by the Swedish team on May 2, we had had six days to wake up and assess our mistakes. We were sure that an absurd accident had made us play so badly, and we were determined not to repeat our flagrant errors from that ill-fated first game. We simply would not repeat our mistakes, that was all.

We would play as a true team, applying a solid zone defense. The forwards would shoot more accurately at Gosta Hogosta's net, and the coaches would not rotate our lines needlessly. What could be simpler?

The next day the newspapers were writing that the goalie Hogosta and the forward Ronald Erickson had together defeated the entire Soviet all-star team. It was incredible! Nothing like that had happened in a world championship series before. We could almost feel the cool gold medals in our palms but we had let the championship go. To be beaten twice by the Swedes was simply hard for me to believe. Our plans were for naught. It seemed as though we had forgotten all our good intentions. We could blame nervousness and the general excitement and commotion, but that was not all. We did not play well in mid-zone and let the Swedes through easily there. We were hesitant about shooting sometimes. Even a veteran like Yakushev, in spite of his usual composure, managed to miss several easy shots into an empty goal.

The Swedes really were magnificent though. Hogosta played like a God. He deserved to be called the best goalie of the championships. Although Erickson drove in all three goals for the Swedes, getting the hat trick, any one of the Swedish forwards rates high praise. Their strategy was effectively executed. They were calculating, smart. It is interesting to note that a psychologist has been actively assisting the Swedish hockey coaches. Maybe he influenced the team's fresh confident play.

For whatever reason, our team—which I considered the strongest—took only third place in the 1977 world championships—not right for the Soviet national team. The

Czechoslovakian team took the gold medal, and the Swedes took the silver to Stockholm.

Our loss may yet be useful to us. It may wake up some of our players: every cloud has a silver lining. We can already see how the fiasco in Vienna has shaken up Soviet hockey. The all-star coaches have been replaced. The structure of club hockey is being polished. Scouts are already rushing out to find young talented skaters. The Federation of Soviet Hockey has undergone a shake-up, and Anotoli Tarasov has been named its vice president.

I am going to the Volga for a rest. I know of one place not far from Saratov where the fishing is wonderful. You just put out a line and the fish bite. I will live in a tent, make chowder, watch the sunrises over the water and think about hockey, about the reasons for our loss in Vienna. In July, I will return home and again go onto the ice.

Epilogue

Hockey will continue. Tournaments, games, warm-ups even—the wheel is turning constantly. I cannot imagine a game other than hockey where such passions boil around a small hard rubber puck. I love this game on the ice, and nothing—even defeats—can extinguish my love for it.

I am 25 years old. How strange it sounds to be called a veteran. Of course, a great deal is behind me now: two Olympiads, seven world championships, five series of games with the professionals in Canada and the United States. For someone else, this would suffice for a lifetime. I, however, am only 25. I am not tired of hockey. With every game, I gain a new edge. I continue to study the game and know more and more about the fine points of hockey. There are no limits. I can study and play the game for a long time yet.

In mastering skills, in every day's anticipation of competition and victory, I sense the purpose of my life: sport. University is behind me. I will probably become a coach eventually, since I enjoy working with boys and watching them improve and gain in daring as well as skill. I might even lecture on the theory and psychology of sports, but whatever my future holds, hockey will have been the brightest part of my life. It will stay with me forever.

I am lucky. I have had a chance to become one of those who opened a new chapter in the history of hockey. I don't doubt that in the future competition between the world's amateurs and professionals will become a common event. This is life's logic. It is inevitable, but it started with us.

Even now, I can hear the howling fans in the Montreal Forum. Our games against the professionals—the Soviet Union vs. the NHL; the Soviet Union vs. the WHA, the Superseries and the Canada Cup—have doubtless been the main events of world-class hockey in recent years.

What lessons have we hockey players learned from these series? First, one has to fight the professionals from the first minute to the last. They do not know fatigue and take advantage of even a minute's weakness in their opponents. One has to be able to resist the hard pressure the professionals exert. In 99 out of 100 cases, the Canadians will be skating all out. It is necessary to expect hard play from the professionals, sometimes dirty play by our Soviet sports standards. When the game gets rough, it is important not to lose self-control, to give the opponents themselves a good scare—better yet, to punish them with a goal. The professionals seem to get rough only when they are behind. Our players may get as many penalties, but we are not out to create a massacre on the ice. Our fans come for the pleasure of the game, not to watch fights.

We have many more meetings with the professionals and with national teams in front of us. I will lower my mask onto my face and skate onto the ice. The rink will be buzzing with anticipation. A whistle will sound, there will be the click of sticks and skates and the game will have begun—the hockey I love.

APPENDIX

International games discussed by Vladislav Tretyak include:
  Soviet Union vs. Team Canada (NHL All-Stars) 1972
  Soviet Union vs. Team Canada (WHA All-Stars) 1974
  Superseries (Central Sports Club of the Army & Soviet Wings vs. 8 NHL
    teams)
  Canada Cup (Canada, Czechoslovakia, Finland, Sweden, US, USSR)
    1976
  World Championships, Vienna (Canada, Czechoslovakia, Finland,
    Romania, Sweden, US, USSR, West Germany) 1977

Although Tretyak also relives the Soviet national championships and other competitions, only the international matches are statistically summarized here.

I. Soviet Union vs. Team Canada (NHL All-Stars) 1972

September 2	Montreal	USSR 7, Canada 3
September 4	Toronto	Canada 4, USSR 1
September 6	Winnipeg	USSR 4, Canada 4
September 8	Vancouver	USSR 5, Canada 3
September 22	Moscow	USSR 5, Canada 4
September 24	Moscow	Canada 3, USSR 2
September 26	Moscow	Canada 4, USSR 3
September 28	Moscow	Canada 6, USSR 5

Standings

	Won	Lost	Tied	Goals For	Goals Against	Points
Canada	4	3	1	31	32	9
USSR	3	4	1	32	31	7

Soviets: Anisin, Blinov, Bodunov, Gusev, Kharlamov, Kuzkin, Lebedev, Liapkin, Lutchenko, Maltsev, Martyniuk, Mikhailov, Mishakov, Paladiev, Petrov, Ragulin, Shadrin, Shatalov, Soludkhin, Starshinov, Tretyak, Tzigankov, Vasiliev, Vikulov, Volchkov, Yakushev, Zimin

Team Canada: Awrey, Berenson, Bergman, Cashman, Clarke, Cournoyer, Dryden, Ellis, P. Esposito, T. Esposito, Gilbert, Goldsworthy, Hadfield, Henderson, D. Hull, Lapointe, F. Mahovlich, P. Mahovlich, Mikita, Parise, Park, Perreault, Ratelle, Redmond, Savard, Seiling, Stapleton, White

II. Soviet Union vs. Team Canada (WHA All-Stars) 1974

September 17	Quebec City	USSR 3, Canada 3
September 19	Toronto	Canada 4, USSR 1
September 21	Winnipeg	USSR 8, Canada 5
September 23	Vancouver	USSR 5, Canada 5
October 1	Moscow	USSR 3, Canada 2
October 3	Moscow	USSR 5, Canada 2
October 5	Moscow	Canada 4, USSR 4
October 6	Moscow	USSR 3, Canada 2

Standings

	Won	Lost	Tied	Goals For	Goals Against	Points
USSR	4	1	3	32	27	11
Canada	1	4	3	27	32	5

Soviets: Anisin, Bodunov, Filippov, Fiodorov, Gusev, Kapustin, Kharlamov, Klimov, Kotov, Kuznetsov, Lebedev, Liapkin, Lutchenko, Maltsev, Mikhailov, Petrov, Polupanov, Popov, Sapelkin, Senadrin, Sidelnikov, Shadrin, Shalimov, Shatalov, Tiruin, Tretyak, Tzigankov, Vasiliev, Vikulov, Volchkov, Yakushev

Team Canada: Backstrom, Bernier, Cheevers, Gratton, Hamilton, Harrison, Henderson, Houle, Gordie Howe, Mark Howe, Marty Howe, Hull, Lacroix, Ley, Macgregor, Mahovlich, McKenzie, McLeod, Selwood, Shmyr, Smith, Stapleton, Tardif, Tremblay, Walton, Webster

III. Superseries 1975—1976

December 28	New York	CSCA 7, RANGERS 3
December 29	Pittsburgh	WINGS 7, PENGUINS 4
December 31	Montreal	CSCA 3, CANADIENS 3
January 4	Buffalo	SABRES 12, WINGS 6
January 7	Chicago	WINGS 4, BLACK HAWKS 2
January 8	Boston	CSCA 5, BRUINS 2
January 10	Uniondale, New York	WINGS 2, ISLANDERS 1
January 11	Philadelphia	FLYERS 4, CSCA 1

Standings	Won	Lost	Tied	Goals For	Goals Against	Points
CSCA	2	1	1	16	12	5
(Central Sports Club of the Army)						
NHL	1	2	1	12	16	3
WINGS	3	1	0	19	19	6
NHL	1	3	0	19	19	2

Combined Standings						
SOVIETS	5	2	1	35	31	11
NHL	2	5	1	31	35	5

Central Sports Club of the Army: Alexandrov, Glazov, Gusev, Kharlamov, Kutyergin, Kuzkin, Lobanov, Lokoto, Lutchenko, Maltsev, Mikhailov, Petrov, Popov, Soludukhin, Tzigankov, Tretyak, Vasiliev, Vikulov, Volchkov, Zhluktov

Soviet Wings: Anisin, Bodunov, Glukov, Gostiuslev, Kapustin, Klimov, Kotov, Krikunov, Kulikov, Kuznetsov, Lapin, Lebedev, Liapkin, Maslov, Rasko, Repniev, Sidelnikov, Shadrin, Shalimov, Tiurin, Yakushev

Black Hawks (Chicago): Bordeleau, Daigle, Espositio, Hull, Koroll, Marks, Martin, Mikita, Mulvey, Murray, Redmond, Rota, Russell, Sheehan, Tallon, White

Bruins (Boston): Bucyk, Cashman, Doak, Edestrand, Forbes, Gibson, Gilbert, Hodge, Marcotte, Nowak, O'Reilly, Park, Ratelle, Savard, Schmautz, Sheppard, Sims, Smith

Canadiens (Montreal): Awrey, Bouchard, Cournoyer, Dryden, Gainey, Jarvis, Lafleur, Lambert, Lapointe, Lemaire, Mahovlich, Riseborough, Roberts, Robinson, Savard, Shutt, Tremblay, Van Boxmeer, Wilson

Flyers (Philadelphia): Barber, Bladon, Bridgman, Clarke, Crisp, Dornhoefer, Dupont, Goodenough, Kelly, Kindrachuk, Leach, Lonsberry, MacLeish, Saleski, Schultz, Stephenson, Van Impe, Jim Watson, Joe Watson

Islanders (New York): Drouin, Fortier, Gillies, Harris, Hart, Henning, Howatt, Lewis, MacMillan, Marshall, Nystrom, Parise, D. Potvin, J. Potvin, Resch, Stewart, St. Laurent, Trottier, Westfall

Penguins (Pittsburgh): Apps, Arnason, Burrows, Campbell, Durbano, Faubert, Gilbertson, Hadfield, Kehoe, Kelly, Larouche, MacDonald, Morrison, Owchar, Plasse, Pronovost, Schock, Stackhouse, Wilkins

Sabres (Buffalo): Desjardins, Fogolin, Gare, Guevrement, Hajt, Korab, Lorentz, Luce, Martin, McNab, Perreault, Ramsay, Richard, Robert, Stanfield, Spencer

IV. Canada Cup 1976

September 2	Ottawa	Canada 11, Finland 2
September 3	Toronto	Sweden 5, US 2
	Montreal	Czechoslovakia 5, USSR 3
September 5	Montreal	Sweden 3, USSR 3
	Toronto	Czechoslovakia 8, Finland 0
	Montreal	Canada 4, US 2
September 7	Montreal	USSR 11, Finland 3
	Philadelphia	Czechoslovakia 4, US 4
	Toronto	Canada 4, Sweden 0
September 9	Winnipeg	Finland 8, Sweden 6
	Philadelphia	USSR 5, US 0
	Montreal	Czechoslovakia 1, Canada 0
September 11	Montreal	US 6, Finland 3
	Quebec City	Sweden 2, Czechoslovakia 1
	Toronto	Canada 3, USSR 1

Final Round
(Best 2 of 3)

September 13	Toronto	Canada 6, Czechoslovakia 0
September 15	Montreal	Canada 5, Czechoslovakia 4, overtime

Standings	Won	Lost	Tied	Goals For	Goals Against	Points
Canada	4	1	0	22	6	8
Czecho-slovakia	3	1	1	19	9	7
Soviet Union	2	2	1	23	14	5
Sweden	2	2	1	16	18	5
United States	1	3	1	14	21	3
Finland	1	4	0	16	42	2

Canada: Barker, Clarke, Dionne, Esposito, Gainey, Gare, Hull, Lafleur, Lapointe, Leach, Mahovlich, Martin, McDonald, Orr, Perreault, Potvin, Robinson, Savard, Shutt, Sittler, Vachon, Watson

Czechoslovakia: Augusta, Bubla, Cernik, Chalupa, Daberle, Dvorak, Dzurilla, Ebermann, Hlinka, Holecek, Holik, Kajkl, Machac, Martinec, Novak, Novy, Pospisil, Pouzar, B. Stastny, M. Stastny, P. Stastny

Soviet Union: Alexandrov, Babinov, Balderis, Belousov, Biljaletdinov, Golikov, Gusev, Kapustin, Kovin, Krikunov, Kulikov, Lebedev, Lutchenko, Maltsev, Repnev, Shalimov, Skvortsov, Tretyak, Vasiliev, Vikulov, Zhluktov

Sweden: Ahlberg, Astrom, Bergman, Brasar, L. Eriksson, R. Eriksson, Hammarstrom, Hedberg, Johansson, Labraaten, Lundstrom, L-G Nilsson, U. Nilsson, Ostling, B. Salming, S. Salming, Sjoberg, Vikstrom, Waltin, Widing

United States: Ahern, C. Bennett, H. Bennett, Bolduc, Chartraw, Christie, Curran, Fogolin, Ftorek, Hangsleben, Jensen, LoPresti, Milbury, Nanne, Noris, Nyrop, O'Flaherty, Palazzari, Patrick, Polich, Sargent, Talafous, Williams

Finland: Flinck, Hagman, Kapanen, Ketola, Koivulshti, Koskinen, Leppanen, Levo, Linnonmaa, Litma, Makkonen, Mattsson, Nummelin, Oksanen, Peltonen, Rautakallio, Rautisainen, Repo, Riihiranta, Rinne, Saari, Tamminen, Vehmanen

V. World Championships, Vienna 1977

April 21	USSR 10	West Germany 0
	Sweden 8	Romania 1
	Czechslovakia 11	Finland 3
	Canada 4	US 1

April 22	US 7	Romania 2
	USSR 11	Finland 6
	Czechoslovakia 9	West Germany 3
	Canada 4	Sweden 2

April 23	Czechoslovakia 13	Romania 1
	Sweden 5	Finland 1
	US 3	West Germany 3
	USSR 11	Canada 1

| April 24 | Sweden 7 | West Germany 1 |
| | USSR 18 | Romania 1 |

| April 25 | Sweden 5 | USSR 1 |
| | Czechoslovakia 6 | US 3 |

| April 26 | Finland 3 | US 2 |
| | Canada 3 | Czechoslovakia 3 |

| April 27 | Canada 5 | Finland 1 |
| | West Germany 6 | Romania 3 |

| April 28 | USSR 6 | Czechoslovakia 1 |
| | Sweden 9 | US 0 |

| April 29 | Canada 9 | West Germany 3 |
| | Finland 4 | Romania 2 |

| April 30 | Czechoslovakia 3 | Sweden 1 |
| | USSR 8 | US 2 |

May 1	Canada 7	Romania 2
	Finland 4	West Germany 1
May 2	Sweden 5	USSR 1
	Czechoslovakia 6	US 3
May 3	Finland 14	Romania 1
	US 4	West Germany 1
May 4	Czechoslovakia 4	USSR 3
	Canada 7	Sweden 0
May 6	Czechoslovakia 2	Sweden 1
	USSR 8	Canada 1
May 8	Canada 8	Czechoslovakia 2
	Sweden 3	USSR 1

Standings

	Won	Lost	Tied
Czechoslovakia	8	2	1
Sweden	7	4	0
USSR	7	4	0
Canada	7	2	1
Finland	4	4	0
US	2	6	1
West Germany	1	6	1
Romania	0	8	0